FORMULA FOR SUCCESS

A Core Concept of Management

OTHER BOOKS BY LAWRENCE A. APPLEY:

Management in Action

The Management Evolution

Values in Management

A Manager's Heritage

FORMULA
FOR
SUCCESS

A Core Concept of

Management

LAWRENCE A. APPLEY

amacom

A Division of American Management Associations

© 1974 AMACOM
A *division of American Management Associations, New York.*
ALL RIGHTS RESERVED. PRINTED IN THE UNITED STATES OF AMERICA.

This publication may not be reproduced, stored in a retrieval system,
or transmitted in whole or in part, in any form or by any means,
electronic, mechanical, photocopying, recording, or otherwise, without
the prior written permission of AMACOM.

International standard book number: 0-8144-5339-2
Library of Congress catalog card number: 73-87546

FIRST PRINTING

DEDICATED

TO

THE AMERICAN MANAGEMENT ASSOCIATIONS

FOREWORD

It will be difficult for any historian to ignore the American Management Associations when writing on the development of management thinking in the twentieth century. Larry Appley has led AMA during most of its years and is symbolic of its growth and prestige. This book represents the high noon of the pioneering movement and the first dawn of management as a profession.

The pioneering movement was marked by a scientific approach to learning about management, mostly through inductive reasoning. Observation indicated that successful managers follow a similar pattern of thought even though their styles are highly personalized. In this book, Larry draws on his career as a top manager in several large corporations and his association with leading managers in large and small organizations. On the basis of these experiences he has confirmed and extended the observations of the pioneers.

The telling contribution of Larry Appley, however, is the knowledge that these fundamental principles can be taught to others. Managers need not be just "born"; they can be "made." This is the discovery that led to the dawn of professional management. Larry established AMA's famous four-week Management Course, one of whose highlights was his own inspirational presentation on the opening day, part of which is embodied in *Formula for Success*. Some twenty thousand managers have been directly influenced by this presentation, and they in turn have influenced innumerable others. Later came the Management Course for Presidents, and from the thousands of chief executives who have participated in it the same message has "cascaded" down into their organizations.

To be heard, language must be simple, clear, and at times didactic. This is the way of the great teacher, and this is the essence of Larry's book. Because the message is so easy to understand and so very difficult to practice, there will always be those who may disagree with an idea here or there. But, after all, pioneers are quick to be critical of each other. Is this not how science advances, and is not the tone of criticism the indicator of professionalism? Society has always benefited from the few who are willing to say what they believe, and never have we needed this kind of book and this kind of writing more than in this day of negativism and nihilism.

I was a member of the four-week AMA Management Course in 1953, so the thoughts in the following pages recall a great source of inspiration in my own life. Moreover, during these past few years I have come to know Larry very well. His adherence to principle, his willingness to listen to new ideas (indeed, encourage them!), and his sensitivity to people and events are familiar to me as an extension of the beliefs he expresses here. This book makes it possible for many who have not had my opportunities to share in a learning experience that I know can bring real change.

Management has been described as "not the doing of things but the development of people." Here we have a handbook for the new manager who wants to learn and a refresher course for the older manager who may have forgotten.

—*James L. Hayes, President*
American Management Associations

viii

PREFACE

It is my humble belief that management has the greatest impact upon human life of any activity, including religion. For many years I said "excluding religion," but I have now become convinced that even religion relies upon good management in order to be effective in human life. It is with considerable humility, therefore, that any single individual should approach the task of reducing to writing his experience and beliefs about such an important activity.

It was my privilege for over eighteen years, as well as a great source of inspiration to me, to stand before the registrants of the Management Course and the Presidents' Course of the American Management Associations on opening day. For years, I found it extremely difficult to convey to the registrants the deep sincerity of my observation that I was offering my thinking and experience for consideration as an illustration and not as "the" way to manage.

My own life has been lived in such a way that I have acquired some deep convictions and have framed some guidelines in connection with my own work. I speak and write at times in what some consider as a domineering, intolerant manner. The members of my own family frequently comment: "Dad may be wrong, but he's never in doubt."

A few years ago, when I was leaving the London airport, John Marsh, president of the British Institute of Management, handed me a precious little book. I read it on the way home and shall always be indebted to John for placing it in my hands.

The book is called *The Human Situation*, and it is a series of Gifford Lectures delivered at the University of Glasgow by W. MacNeile Dixon during 1935 to 1937. The very first page expressed my sentiments so perfectly that I have quoted it many times since. It reads as follows: *

> The best we can do, the most I can promise you, is to employ familiar words, the words of our daily speech, and to use them in the sense in which we are all accustomed. I shall abide, as far as I can, by the tradition of our country and our ancestors. . . .
>
> I propose to speak my mind. I cannot believe you would wish me to say what I did not think or think what I did not say. Nothing is to be gained by concealment or equivocation. If you find my conclusions unpalatable, you are not without resource. You have only to assure yourselves that I am totally mistaken, which may, indeed, very likely be the truth. And—who knows?—I may learn wisdom, and come to think differently. I would have you regard these occasions as conversations. My views will be at your disposal for consideration, not necessarily for acceptance. If they have no inherent persuasiveness, I would not have you accept them. There are in the realm of thought no absolute authorities, no dictators. No man, living or dead, can claim oracular powers. Mine is a personal view. All philosophies are in the end personal. You can no more escape your philosophy than you can escape your own shadow, for it also is a reflection of yourself.

*Reprinted with the permission of St. Martin's Press, Inc., Edward Arnold Ltd.

Systems of thought are the shadows cast by different races, epochs and civilizations.

> China and Ind, Hellas and France,
> Each hath its own inheritance;
> And each to Truth's rich market brings
> Its bright, divine imaginings.

All reasoning is in a manner biased, and the bias is due to the nature, surroundings and education of the thinker. We are none of us merely logical or calculating machines. Mathematical reasoning is more nearly impersonal than any other type, but, as Aristotle pointed out, you do not ask it of the stateman. And the matters with which we are to deal are not susceptible of mathematical demonstration.

The key thoughts in this quotation are: "I would have you regard these occasions as conversations"; "my views will be at your disposal for consideration, not necessarily for acceptance"; "if they have no inherent persuasiveness, I would not have you accept them"; and "mine is a personal view."

It is my plea, therefore, that you read the contents of this book with the thought in mind that I am simply sharing some ideas and experiences for what they are worth to the reader. They are offered neither as authoritative nor exclusive. *They are intended to be purely thought-provoking.*

Lawrence A. Appley

CONTENTS

Anyone with the determination and skill to do so can accomplish anything within reason. Determination and skill increase the range of reasonableness.

Chapter 1

A CORE CONCEPT OF MANAGEMENT IN BRIEF FORM

Life need not be complicated if we live it by simple truths. It is only complicated when we make it so.

Purposeful action is more gratifying than aimless busyness. If one wishes to, there are ways to make the future, rather than wait for it. There are means for making things happen rather than letting them happen. Living creatively seems more beneficial to one's fellow men than just existing.

It is possible for an individual to move toward the attainment of a preestablished objective rather than let each day take care of itself. He cannot always do this singlehandedly and, therefore, must exert influence upon the efforts of others. This separates him from the followers and makes him a leader.

The core concept of management is this: *Management is getting things done through other people*. Management, therefore, becomes any activity which involves leading *any*

1

group of people toward the attainment of common objectives in any walk of life.

The management concept as just stated is not a new one. This particular statement of it is of undisclosed origin that can be traced back, at least, to the late 19th century.

The implication of this concept is that he who does things himself is an individual producer and not a manager. He is not getting things done; he is doing them. The manner in which one gets things done through others differs in every respect from the way in which one does things himself. He who is expert in individual productivity is not necessarily effective in attaining high individual productivity from others, nor is there any basic requirement that he be one in order to do the other.

Management is an activity in itself, unlike any other activity, and it is founded upon certain basic principles, responsive to an orderly approach, dependent upon unique skills and tools, guided by a code of ethics, and controlled by disciplines. He who would be an effective professional manager must be a continuing student of the principles, skilled in the art, and master of the tools; he must practice high ethical standards and self-discipline.

"He who can manage can manage anything." When that statement was made back in the 1930s, the speaker was considered to be a bit "balmy." In those days the head of an oil company must have been born and raised in an oil well and have crude oil running out of his ears and nose. To be the head of a telephone company, he must have worked at some time in his life on a pole, as well as in other activities that enabled him to know the business "from the ground up." Technical knowledge was paramount.

It is now realized, however, that management knowledge is more important than technical knowledge. It is expected that a manager will select competent specialists and that his talent will be based upon his ability to cordinate their efforts. He does not have to be a specialist to manage specialists.

2

When General Brehon B. Somerville retired from the Army after World War II, he became the chief executive officer of Kopper Co., Inc., the coke manufacturer. He had spent his entire career in military service. There were those who wondered how he could head up a coke company without knowing something about coke, its derivatives, and uses. (He frankly admitted that he thought it came in a bottle.)

When asked why he thought he could be head of a coke company, he replied, "Why shouldn't I?" He was then told that he should know all about coke, and all the processes in connection with it, to be successful. His response was, "I'll hire specialists who know the technology required." The next question put to him was, "How do you know when you have the right specialists?" His response was, "I can't lay an egg, but I can smell a rotten one."

One does not have to be a doctor to know that he has a good one. One does not have to be a school teacher to know that her children are being taught well. One does not have to be a carpenter to know that his house is being built well. Were this required, it would be impossible of achievement because no chief executive could be a specialist in all of the areas of specialization that he is required to coordinate.

He who can manage can manage anything! In order to do so, however, he must know how to act like a manager in any situation calling for management, for leadership. He must know:

I. The Nature of Leadership
   A. Leadership means action—getting things done through other people.
   B. Professional leadership means purposeful action.
   C. Action requires thought.
   D. The future requires more thought than the past.
II. The Processes of Leadership
   A. Determine where we are now. (Inventory)
   B. Determine what we want people to do. (Planning)

C. Determine the people needed to do it. (Organize Human Resources)

D. Determine what the people need to do it. (Organize Physical Resources)

E. Determine how well people should do it. (Standards of Performance)

F. Determine how well they do it. (Progress Review)

G. Determine what help people need to do better. (Development and Controls)

H. Determine what we will pay. (Rewards and Incentives)

III. The Character in Leadership

A. Leaders have records of attainment.

B. Leaders have a mission.

C. Leaders use consultative supervision.

D. Leaders are intellectually mature.

E. Leaders are emotionally stable.

Years ago, leaders commonly referred to their understudies as follows: "I came up the hard way, let him do likewise." The training of potential leaders was questioned because of the expressed danger of identifying crown princes or of establishing a class of fair-haired boys. All of this was a compromise with reality and an evasion of responsibility. It was ridiculing the inevitable.

Hand-me-down training (from father to son, from boss to subordinate) was the order of the day. When son learns from father and a subordinate learns from his boss, without the benefit of other training and inspiration, a dilution in competency takes place. If out of such a process the student is any better than the teacher, it is due to superior capability of the student that conquers despite the limitations of the process.

As a result, most leaders today have learned management by exposure and experience, and each day is a round of busyness rather than an orderly, skilled process of attainment.

Legal training is not leadership training. Training to be an engineer, a clergyman, a physicist, an educator, or a politician makes very little contribution to management capability.

It is to be noted that I am using leadership and management interchangeably. Unfortunately, management has too exclusively been identified with business and industrial activity, where human beings are gathered together in a group for the attainment of some particular objective. Management is to be found in the home, in the church, government, labor unions, information media, professional services, and on the farm, as well as in business and in industry.

The problems facing us today and the anticipated and unanticipated problems of the future are so massive and so grim that the finest of leadership is required to meet them, and leadership is not of the finest unless it is highly trained, skilled, and scientific.

Most leaders today are selected by chance, are victims of circumstances, or are the products of extremely unscientific selection processes. They happened to be in a certain place at a certain time when a leader was being selected, and some particular coincidence or circumstance swept them into the vacuum that ultimately blew them to the top.

Strong, dynamic, competent, enlightened leadership makes things happen. It shapes and makes the future. It develops trends, initiates change, and influences environment. It creates opportunity rather than becoming a victim of circumstance.

For the last forty years in general, and for the last ten years in particular, I have researched and inquired; I have observed and studied; I have pled and argued in an effort to find out whether our professional educators had any intention of teaching or competency to teach men and women how to act like leaders in situations requiring leadership action. Time has run out on such observations as: "Leaders are born and not made." "Leadership is what the man is and this cannot be taught." "There is no 'discipline' of management that can be taught."

5

It is perfectly fantastic in a world that wants peace, in a world where there is an instrument like the United Nations that can bring about world peace, that there has not been the leadership available to keep the world at peace.

It is incredible that a wall has been built right through the middle of a city in modern times and people have been killed for trying to get over, under, or through it. It is beyond one's comprehension that a nation can cost human life and create human despair through attempts by others to contain its aggressiveness. It is beyond the belief of modern man that a single individual can subjugate the people of a small island and threaten the accepted way of life of two continents. The rioting in the cities, the crime on the streets, revolutions on our campuses, bulging mental institutions, and broken homes are products of a vacuum in dynamic, skilled, trained leadership.

Leaders can be trained; they can be trained for leadership in the church, the government, the school, the labor union, in business, in industry, and in any other segment of human endeavor. It takes time, effort, and money. It also will save time, effort, and money. At least one idea of the outline of such training is presented here. If any individuals or any institutions are to acquire a depth of conviction that leads to action along these lines, it is for them to determine the subject matter and the processes. My experience dictates to me, however, that what follows will be effective.

Training for leadership should consist of study, drill, examination, and certification in the following areas, at least:

1. The nature of management.
2. The processes of management.
3. The character *in* management.

Chapter 2

THE NATURE OF
MANAGEMENT

It seems desirable that people in management should be able to define specifically and explain clearly just what the activity is in which they are engaged. A doctor rather quickly can define and explain medicine. A labor leader knows and can tell you immediately what the labor movement is. Being able to define what occupies a good part of our lives gives tone, purpose, and challenge to gainful employment.

Management Is a Profession

Many respected authorities have examined and written on the subject of the basic qualifications an activity must meet in order to be recognized as a profession. Among these is the Committee for Economic Development. Some years ago, the committee preceded one of its studies with such a list.

In reading these various opinions and findings, I have been able to trace five basic qualifications which seem to appear, in one form or another, throughout most of them.

7

They are as follows. An activity in order to qualify as a profession must have:

1. A body of knowledge that can be taught.
2. A scientific approach.
3. Skills and tools.
4. A code of ethics.
5. Discipline.

Management, as an activity, readily falls under that classification.

In any profession, there are *certain known facts and principles* that have been discovered by predecessors with which present members of the profession do not have to experiment. Each generation of the profession contributes something to the body of known facts. Progress in the effectiveness of the profession would be greatly reduced if each member of it had to discover for himself all principles and facts affecting the work he has to do.

The young lawyer, doctor, or engineer undergoes years of study in order to discover what his predecessors have proved to be fact. With those items thus covered, he does not have to experiment and he has no reason to doubt their accuracy. In other words, his predecessors have furnished a foundation upon which he can work and build.

In the February 19, 1973, issue of *Industry Week* is an article titled "Is Management a Profession?" This article quotes authorities which cause the writer of the article to summarize as follows: "So we've come full circle from strong assertions that management is a profession, to hopes it will become one, to strong beliefs that it is not and never will be a profession."

A professor of management at one of our prominent universities is quoted as saying, "We don't really know anything about management. You look at what the curriculums are and its a hodge-podge. We really don't know what we mean by management. Over the years of study, with all the talk

8

of leadership and decision making . . . when it gets down to it my Mother, rest her soul, had all the conventional wisdom necessary. . . . You can be a doctor and a hospital administrator. You can be an engineer and a manager. You superimpose management over an expertise. So the question is, is there expertise in management itself? I think it's a nonconcept."

It is my sincere hope that the author of that statement reads this book. Forty-five years of studying, practicing, and teaching management enables me to discern the lack of knowledge displayed. What exists in our universities and colleges on the subject of management is no criterion of what exists. There is today a large body of organized, evaluated management knowledge that can be taught. There is a discipline. When Courtney Brown was dean of the Columbia Graduate School of Business he made the statement, in an important address, that "Management has now taken its place alongside of theology, education, medicine, law, and engineering as one of the great professions of the world." What a discerning and accurate statement that was!!

Professional management is purposeful action. It is the difference between action that can be characterized as pure busyness and action that seems to be directed toward attainment of something. "Education without action is futile. Action without education is fatal." Professional management is the attainment of a predetermined objective by guiding human, mental, and physical effort toward that end.

If management is a profession, then it follows that there are numerous facts and principles which predecessors in the profession have discovered to be true—facts and principles with which young people taking over management responsibilities do not have to tamper, experiment, or compromise. Imagine a doctor trying to cure human beings without years of basic training. Yet, observe men trying to *develop and direct* human beings without training. If a doctor needs years to learn how to cure people, it would seem reasonable that

9

a manager or supervisor should require at least a few months to learn how to develop people.

It is not uncommon practice to select for a sales manager an employee who has been a loyal, hardworking salesman, with twelve or fifteen years of service, who knows markets, prices, policies, products, and consumer buying habits backwards and forwards, and who can outsell anybody else in the organization. Because of this knowledge and these personal qualifications, he is made a sales manager with very little other preparation for it. In such cases, the point is ignored that *there is just as much to be known about managing salesmen as there is about selling*. That employee is entering a profession for which he is unprepared. He is in much the same position as a young man trying to practice medicine without having been trained to be a doctor.

This situation can be duplicated in the machine shop, in the accounting department, on the transportation lines, and in practically every phase of any organization; and yet, there is a fund of information concerning well-established facts and principles which is practically fatal for a person in a supervisory or managerial position to ignore.

When a man is called upon to manage, and has no other preparation than technical knowledge and skill, it takes much native ability to be successful. It is largely a matter of chance if he has it. The chance for failure is, of course, now being reduced by the increasing number of trained executives and supervisors around him. The standards are rising; the pressure is greater.

If a new executive does not happen to stumble upon correct methods of management, he begins to run into difficulties, develops complexes; and out of such a situation, you may get a hard-boiled, rule-of-thumb manager whose method is dictation, whose word is law, and who finds support only by using force and authority. Many of the individuals who have cracked up in the face of executive responsibility have wanted to operate correctly, but have not known how. Not being prepared and trained in proper methods, they adopt those which are the easiest and which ultimately result in failure.

There is no profession about which all that can be known *is* known. In every profession, there is still a broad field of experimentation. Activities coming within that field should be identified as such. It is in that field that present members of the profession have an opportunity to make contributions. It is in that field that they discover new truths and add such discoveries to the growing volume of known facts. All available human ability and ingenuity must be concentrated in the area of the unknown. Why waste effort arguing about or compromising with truths that already have been discovered for us? The doctor, the engineer, and the lawyer have these two fields of the known and the unknown definitely segregated in their own minds. Why should not people in positions of management and supervision be fortified to the same extent? It seems too great a risk to leave able administration to happy accident.

It may be limiting to identify management as a profession. It is also an art and a science. It is an art because it requires certain specific aptitudes and skills. It is a science because there is a great body of knowledge available and there are established principles to guide its basic activities. It is probably best, therefore, to identify the activity of management as a profession, an art, and a science.

Streamlining is a term that has increased in usage during recent years and is generally conceived as applying to the shape of some tangible article. It is interesting to realize that intangibles—such as attitudes, thinking processes, conditions, and situations—may also be streamlined.

The purpose of streamlining is to reduce resistance to forces which cannot themselves be changed. Such forces are commonly thought of as wind, water, and other phenomena over which human beings have little influence. Actual reduction of resistance usually takes the form of changing the shape and the lines so as to pass more easily through, or take advantage of, natural and inevitable forces.

There are definite trends in human activities, attitudes, and conditions which are just as inevitable as the wind and the rain. They move on in increasing tempo regardless of the wishes of any particular individual. These trends are developed as the result of practices and attitudes of human beings.

An illustration is that of the trend toward mass production. Economic conditions, changes and extensions in markets, increased demands, the necessity for higher standards of living, have made mass production and the assembly line a necessity. Some economists and businessmen fought it, social organizations cried out against it, but its continuation seems to be certain and efforts should be directed toward controlling it in the best interests of all.

Another trend that is beginning to take definite shape at this time is the trend toward professional management. Trade and professional associations, civic clubs, educational institutions, business and industrial executives, and government administrators are studying this trend with deep interest.

Professional management is sweeping across the economic and industrial world with such inevitable force that no one person can stop it regardless of his personal reaction. It would seem that individuals, not wishing to be checked or swept aside in their progress, would study growing trends and would streamline their attitudes and activities in order to reduce resistance to these trends. The modern executive is studying administrative processes as never before. He is analyzing the fundamentals that administrative practice has established as sound and is conducting experiments in the field of the unknown.

Each person in a position of supervision over other people is faced with making a decision as to whether he will direct his activities on the basis of careful planning and sound control. If he decides to ignore the advisability of planning and setting up proper control media, then he must fight the trend toward better administration.

Management Defined

Management is the responsibility for accomplishing results through the efforts of other people. Further investigation discloses that there are many synonyms for the word: administration, supervision, foremanship, and leadership. Management refers to any individual having responsibility for the activities of others, whether he be the chief executive of an organization with 10,000 people, or a group leader with only three or four people under his direction.

The definition just offered is a brief one. Some have made it even more brief by stating it as follows: *Management is getting things done through people.* There is a longer definition which happens to be my favorite. It was developed by a group of business executives and teachers of business administration, who met for an entire weekend at the Schenley Hotel in Pittsburgh back in 1941, for the purpose of arriving at a common definition. With some slight change that has taken place with usage, the definition is as follows:

> *Management is guiding human and physical resources into dynamic organization units which attain their objectives to the satisfaction of those served and with a high degree of morale and sense of attainment on the part of those rendering the service.*

These definitions are offered purely for the purpose of illustration. Many other definitions from accepted authorities in the field of management are available. The principle stated here is that those in management should be able to define it. They should become acquainted with the best definitions that are available and, from these, form their own. There are many features of all definitions that are common. The definitions offered here are not offered as the most acceptable ones. They just happen to be those that I personally like and present as thought-provoking.

Management makes things happen. Management does not wait for the future; it makes the future. Managers are not custodians of the present; they are architects of the future. Nicholas Murray Butler once said: "There are three kinds of people in this world: Those who make things happen; those who watch things happen; and those who do not know what's happening." Managers are supposed to be in the first group.

If a manager wishes to know how effective he is, let him list those things that have happened in the last twelve months because he made them happen. Is the line of products and services different? Are the costs any lower? Are the sales any higher? Is the profit any greater? Are the people any finer? Is the morale any better? Is the place any cleaner? Is he conscious of having any impact upon his environment and what takes place within it?

Frederick R. Kappel, former president and chairman of the board of American Telephone & Telegraph Company, spoke at Westminster College in Fulton, Missouri, in 1962. Mr. Kappel said this: "To have a part in significant enterprise, to be one of its movers and managers—in industry or in government—is not to fill some niche each morning and leave it each night as you found it. It is to help build and shape, to plan and to execute, to measure alternatives against the horizon and act on the course that judgment and resolution commend."

On the front page of the August 1968 issue of the American Appraisal Company's *Clients' Service Bulletin,* we read:

> It is a part of human nature to hope for something lucky to happen, some facet of fortune that will give one an unforeseen advantage, a boost ahead. Sometimes such a chance occurs, but it is well to remember that success

never comes to a man of its own volition. The ease and rapidity of success seldom just happen in this world—it must be brought about. The man who wishes to attain leadership must everlastingly develop and sustain an insatiable desire to satisfy his disciplined curiosity about his world and a painstakingly active determination to put across whatever plan of life he envisions.

Leaders think, act, and motivate. Followers do, object to, resist, or revolt against what leaders do.

There is one truth that has been learned by thousands of executives and supervisors which has a decided effect upon their administrative attitudes and practices. Its acceptance or rejection divides administrators into two distinct groups. If accepted soon enough in an administrator's experience, it saves considerable grief. The principle is this: Management is *not* the direction of things, it *is* the development of people.

Management is taking people as they are, with what knowledge, training, experience, and background they have accumulated, and developing those people by increasing their knowledge, improving their skills, and correcting their habits and attitudes. Upon this improvement depends the success of any managerial or supervisory effort. In terms of such improvement, executive ability can be measured.

Put this principle to the test. Try to think of any activity with which you are dealing that does not involve the development of people: idle buildings; cold, uninteresting budgets; action to be approved such as appropriations, requisitions, capital expenditures; analysis of statistics—all require the selection, the training, and the supervision of people in order that these activities may be handled properly.

Action Requires Thought

One of the greatest tragedies in management circles is that leaders do not spend sufficient time thinking—thinking about the responsibilities, obligations, and practices of their respective positions. Thought controls action, and a manager does what he thinks. He may not do all that he thinks, but he cannot do what he does not think.

It would appear sometimes that action is instantaneous and there is no time for thought to precede it. If one were to bring his finger in contact with an electric current, he would withdraw it instantly. He cannot do so, however, until his mind has told him to, and this mental image is transmitted through his motor nerves to his fingertips. If, perchance, there is not time enough between contact with the "hot" wire and the action required to let go of it, then one cannot let go and one dies.

Ayn Rand, author of *The Fountainhead, Atlas Shrugged,* and *For the New Intellectual,* has one of the most stimulating minds I have ever met. I cannot accept her basic philosophy in its entirety and I am sure she would not expect this. I do, however, admire the way in which her mind works. Following is a quotation from *Atlas Shrugged*:

> Man's mind is his basic tool of survival. Life is given to him; survival is not. His body is given to him; its sustenance is not. His mind is given to him; its content is not. To remain alive, he must act and before he can act, he must know the nature and the purpose of his action. He cannot obtain his food without a knowledge of food and the way to obtain it. He cannot dig a ditch or build a cyclotron without a knowledge of his aim and the means to achieve it. To remain alive, he must think.

Albert Schweitzer, when asked what is wrong with the world today, answered quickly: "Man simply does not think. The greatest discovery of any generation is that human beings can alter their lives by altering their attitudes of mind." Blaise Pascal, the French philosopher who lived from 1623 to 1662, included in his writings: "Man's greatness lies in his power of thought."

Dr. Cary Middlecoff, twice National Open Golf Champion of the United States, says: "It does no good to think of what you should have done after you have hit a foolish shot. Good golf requires good thinking, as well as good swinging—and the former will bring on the latter."

Dr. James Bonner, Cal Tech professor of biology, observes: "A better quality of man is going to be necessary if the species is to survive in the world men have made. That means educating every human brain to use it effectively. Biologists believe a tenfold increase in this brain usage is entirely possible—perhaps even imperative."

"When I pause longest, I make the most telling strokes with my brush," said Leonardo da Vinci. "That society is great whose men of business think greatly of their function" is a quotation from Alfred North Whitehead and is inscribed at the entrance of the Columbia Graduate School of Business.

James Allen once wrote: "As you think, you travel. You are today where your thoughts have brought you, and you will be tomorrow where your thoughts take you. Whatever your present environment may be, you will fall, remain, or rise with your thoughts, your wisdom, your ideal. You will become as small as your controlling desire and as great as your dominant aspiration."

The basic nature of management requires that its first step be thought. If management is getting other people to do things, then the leader must know what he wishes other people to do. This requires training and a capacity to develop a clear, mental image of exactly what we wish to have done.

The development of such a mental image of action we would like to have taken by others is enhanced by discussion with others. If one of the great tragedies of modern management is that it does not think enough, the second great tragedy is that we do not talk enough.

The strong silent type is no longer the effective type. Well do I remember an executive who sat by the hour, the day, and the month behind his desk or in meetings, puffing away on his massive pipe. He always had before him a large box of matches and he would strike matches and light his pipe continually. He seldom talked. There was an impression on the part of his associates that a massive brain was working away strenuously as the smoke came forth in profuse amounts. It was some years before his associates discovered that all he was doing was smoking.

An individual could spend hours and days with himself, thinking about certain action he would like to take. He could read all that is available to him; he could study; he could think his best and uninterrupted thoughts. In due time, he is prepared with his finest solution.

As this man comes out into the open after his seclusion during the thinking process, he meets a taxi driver. The driver asks him what he has been doing and he says, "Thinking." "Thinking about what?" asks the taxi driver. As the man begins to tell the driver what he was thinking about, his thinking gets clearer.

Later in the office, he meets a fellow executive who knows nothing about the subject matter. When the thinker begins to tell this colleague what he has been thinking about, the colleague begins to ask questions for further clarification. This aids the thinking process—having to answer another's questions. In due time, he meets a specialist on the subject matter and they exchange views, and this specialist makes contributions to the thinking. One cannot help ending with a better result than he had at the completion of his own isolated thinking.

If thinking out a mental image of action to be taken is done in discussion with others, and particularly with those who are to take the action, a very interesting development occurs. Those who have participated in the discussion are part of the final conclusion and are committed to its successful execution. This provides a very high degree of motivation.

Why should managers spend a considerable amount of time thinking about management and how they practice it?

Effective practice requires a clear, concise, orderly, and precise concept of exactly what management is. One must be continually reexamining, reaffirming, or modifying his concept. It must, however, be clear at all times if he is to be an outstanding manager, a leader who has followers. Leadership requires followership, and followership is usually attracted by a leader who knows where is going and how he is going to get there.

It is my sincere hope that a student of this material, whether he reads it or hears it, will fully comprehend the power that it implies. Visualize, if you will, a leader of a management team, each individual member of which has a different concept from what he has and from what other members of the team have as to how the team should work together and how the enterprise should be managed. If each has a little different mental concept, there is confusion, misunderstanding, and internal conflict when action is required.

If, on the other hand, there is uniform agreement and, therefore, there are uniform mental images in the minds of all members of the team, the results have to be far more positive than otherwise. Fred Lazarus, Jr., of the Federated Stores, headquartered in Cincinnati, Ohio, says: "All members of the team must dance to the same music, play the same tune." This does not mean that he wants a team of yes men. It means that a management team, like an orchestra, has to be following the same melody. Each member may play a different instrument and play a different part, but if they are all playing the same composition, the result is harmony.

As one visualizes this kind of situation, there comes into his mind numerous orchestra leaders. It is well known that some are more effective than others, and it is known that different leaders have varying success with the same orchestras. This is entirely dependent upon the skill of the leader to get the members of the orchestra to play their parts with skill, with enthusiasm, and with a spirit of complete cooperation.

19

It should be clear by now that the author believes, with some degree of conviction, that managers should think, that they should think in consultation and discussion with other thinkers, and that they should think out clear, mental images of how they want to manage, why they should manage that way, and how they can be most effective.

The Future Requires More Thought Than the Past

Why is it necessary that managers do more thinking than they ever have done in the past? Why is so much emphasis being placed upon it at this time? It is because the problems that management faces are becoming more and more difficult, and they are becoming more difficult more rapidly than ever before in history. The increasing magnitude of our problems and the stepped-up rate in their development are an inherent part of progress in civilization.

Progress in civilization, to me, means human development—improvement in the stature, character, and capability of individual human beings. This can take place only in an environment of tougher and tougher competition. One cannot improve his tennis by always playing someone he can defeat. One's bridge game never will improve if one always wins. A skilled runner will run faster, the faster his competition. If man is to develop, the problems he faces must be increasingly difficult with each generation.

The rate, nature, speed, and certainty with which change is taking place and problems are developing in modern civilization are now being expressed by the word "explosion." There is the population explosion, the information explosion, the education explosion, technology explosion, management explosion, and so on and on. Let us turn our attention to a few of these.

(This text is being written in a most unorthodox way. Academically, there should be evidence of the qualification of the writer by the presence of footnotes and references indicating sources of information. Were I to write a text in that fashion, it never would be written. Fortunately, or otherwise, I am too busy *living* in management to find the time to meet the requirements of full-time writers for putting together a book.

(During forty years of experience in management, I have made the thinking, the writing, and the activities of other people a part of myself. Many, many great quotations come to my mind and I frequently cannot identify the origin of them. Certain statements I am about to make are believed, by me, to be facts which I have gathered from appropriate authorities, but I would be at a loss to tell you who the authorities are, or when I came across the information. The purpose of the information is the impact it has upon the reader. While the statistics may not be exactly correct, the import of them is, I am sure, quite accurate.)

THE TECHNOLOGY EXPLOSION

There has been more technological discovery in the last twenty-odd years than in all of mankind's history to that time. I do not know how old man is, but there is some general agreement that he has been on this earth for millions of years. More knowledge has been developed in the last twenty-five years of his existence than in all the previous millions.

Look what has happened to the speed of man! It took him from the Garden of Eden until 1950 to attain the fantastic speed of 740 miles an hour. Twenty years later, he was traveling at more than 27,000 miles an hour.

Consider the explosive power available to man. He started out with his bare fists. He got himself a slingshot, a bow and arrow, a catapult, then gunpowder. In the year 1800, the standard measurement of explosive power was two pounds of black gunpowder. In 1950, it was one ton of TNT. Today the standard measurement of explosive power is one megaton, or one million tons of TNT. More explosive power can be loaded on one bomber than was fired in all of World War II by both sides.

Sixty percent of all the technical knowledge available to mankind has been discovered in the last twenty-five years. Ninety percent of all the scientists who ever lived are now alive. Some authority has said that if one wished to keep up with the development of new technical knowledge, he would have to take a four-year college course every four years. It has been said that a college sophomore today has to know more about the nucleus than Niels Bohr knew about it at the time he received the Nobel Prize for it more than fifty years ago.

What does this fantastic development of technological know-how mean to management? It means that all that management has to do is to adapt this technical know-how to the good of mankind rather than for his destruction. This is no job for an amateur; it will take a professional.

THE HUMAN EXPLOSION

Wherever you find human beings, they automatically divide themselves into followers and leaders. They have various processes for doing this, but it always ends that way. I like to call them "The Masses" and "The Few."

In my humble opinion The Masses have three interesting characteristics: they resist change; they must change; and they are under tremendous pressure to change. Let us examine these characteristics in that order.

Resistance to change. Arthur ("Red") H. Motley, president of Parade Publications, Inc., and former president of the U.S. Chamber of Commerce, has said: "Nothing happens until somebody sells something." The farmers still would be plowing their fields with oxen if someone had not sold them modern farm machinery. Clerks still would be writing with quill pens if someone had not sold them on modern office equipment. Housewives still would be scrubbing their clothes on the river bank if someone had not convinced them to use automatic washing machines and driers. People are basically creatures of habit. They want to be left alone.

Possibly, you have been acquainted with what is commonly called a commuter. Stuart Chase of the *Reader's Digest* once defined New York City as "that place where people are pumped back and forth between places where they would rather not live and places they would rather not work." We are told that these human automatons are made this way by "the establishment," "the organization." Please do not be misled; they are *born* that way.

Consider, if you will, a commuter who has been taking the 7:53 every morning for twenty-five years. He arrives at the station, finds the mark on the edge of the platform that he has worn with the edge of his shoe all these years, and stands there waiting for the steps of his car to stop right in front of him. If they do not happen to stop right in front of him, he will walk right into the side of the car. After he gets in the half-empty car, he discovers someone sitting in *his* seat. He blows tobacco smoke into the man's face and scowls until he moves.

Our commuter then sits down and folds his newspaper in exactly the same way he has been doing for twenty-five years. He reads it the same way. First, he looks in the obituaries to see if he is still alive. Then, he looks at the financial page to see if he is still solvent. Then, he avidly reads the sports page to see if he won those bets he made at lunch the day before. He will then read the front page and catch up with all the crime, corruption, politics, wars, and murders. He might spend two or three minutes with the editorial section since that is all the intellectual stimulation this creature of habit can stand.

If my history properly advises me, missionaries are not welcome among the heathen of Central Africa. They want to be left alone. And many social workers know how discouraging a slum clearance project can be. Too often, when the occupants of a slum move into a new housing development, they take the slum right with them.

They must change. Progress in civilization demands that "The Masses" change their habits even though they resist it. There must be continuing improvement in their lot in life. Even though they enjoy the circumstances within which they live, primarily because they have never known anything else, society says they cannot continue with the status quo.

Pressure to change. Because communication has become instantaneous, "The Masses" are under fantastic pressure to change. It gives one a pounding headache to think about it. Anything that is going on in the world today can be made known to the rest of the world simultaneously. Possibly, you had the experience of watching a world TV program on which a Picasso masterpiece was being auctioned for charity. Audiences in London, Paris, New York, Fort Worth, and Los Angeles were bidding on the masterpiece exactly as though they were in the same room together.

Half a century ago, there could have been a revolution on a college campus and that would have been the end of it. It would have taken so long for the news to reach other campuses that they would have lost interest. The great civil rights demonstrations would not have taken place, but today, it is possible for someone to stand on the courthouse steps of a segregated community and appeal to the world to come to the rescue and the world hears about it. A housewife boycotts a supermarket in Detroit and it spreads throughout the nation. A ruinous riot takes place in one of our great cities, and the next night riots start in other cities.

We are puzzled by the reaction of some of our youths to war. When we went off to previous wars, we marched in our clean khaki behind the village band and our friends and relatives said good-bye at the station as we boarded the troop train swathed in flags and banners. Months or years later, we came back minus a leg, an arm, an eye, and sometimes in a wheelchair—but still in clean khaki with ribbons on

24

our chests. Nobody but the veterans knew what happened while they were away. Today, the blood of war runs in color in our living rooms. It is not an inviting sight.

Most poverty-stricken homes in our ghettoes have TV sets. Victims of poverty sit in front of these sets all day, listening to what Americans should wear, what Americans should drive, what Americans should smoke and drink, what Americans should live in—hour after hour, they are pounded with what they should have. Ultimately, they are driven to have it and if they can't earn it, they steal it.

"The Masses" are creatures of habit and do not want to change. They have to change, however, and are being pressured to change because of the communications media that develop and increase the pressure.

"The Few"—the leaders, according to this purely personal analysis—divide themselves into two groups: those who deny "The Masses" the right to choose the nature of the change they are to make, and those who provide "The Masses" with an opportunity to choose the change they are going to make. It is not difficult to identify these people in any leadership situation. They are not only heads of states; they can be found in the home, in the church, in the school, in the government, in labor unions, in business, and in industry.

Those who deny "The Masses" freedom of choice regarding the change they are to make do so in order to *exploit* the people for some selfish reason. It is their desire to take advantage of the people. They, therefore, have to lull them into insensitivity, and for this they have a theme song.

The theme song goes something like this: "Share according to your need." This tells the people to quit worrying, to take it easy, and be taken care of. Juvenal, a Roman satirist of the second century, said, "Two things only the people anxiously desire—bread and circuses." Ultimately, people on the receiving end of a soothing treatment of this kind wake up to find that they are well taken care of, but they have lost all individuality or sense of attainment.

Richard Goodwin, helper of at least two United States

presidents in the development of political terms and slogans, has said: "The coercive society is no less obnoxious when coercion is masked in benevolence." That, in my humble opinion, is an extremely profound, potent, and intelligent observation.

Those who give "The Masses" a choice regarding the change they would like to make do so in order to *develop* the people. Those who choose their own destiny are stronger for it. They may or may not be as well off personally, but they can live with themselves.

Those who permit "The Masses" to make their own decisions also have a theme song they sing: "Share according to your contribution." It is my humble opinion that this theme song would be more popular that the former one if the disc jockeys played it more. Those in positions of influence, however, frequently feel their positions are more secure when they soothe the people rather than challenge them.

What does this mean in the way of a challenge to management? It means in a day and age when work is being questioned, as to the need for it as well as the dignity and the respectability of it, managers have to get people to work, to work hard, to work well, and to work willingly. This is no job for an amateur; it takes a professional.

Richard Goodwin, quoted earlier, said at the same time: "Modern America assaults the deepest values of our civilization, those worlds within a world where each can find meaning and dignity of work."

James R. Bierly, president of Mansfield Brass & Aluminum, says: "Work can and should be challenging, creative, stimulating, and rewarding. It is my intention to make it so in our company."

Dr. Merritt B. Low, president of the Massachusetts chapter of the American Academy of Pediatrics in Greenfield, Massachusetts, said in a personal letter to me, referring to a meeting we had both attended, "One last oar that I wanted to get in but time forbade it, was the concept that 'work' has become a loaded, escalated word for those 'who do' and those 'who don't'—and perhaps as we take in new thoughts and phrases in the give and take of the group, we should think of terms like achievement, contribution, commitment as replacements for that dirty, tarnished four-letter word—*work*."

Just in case anybody is thinking at this point that it might be difficult to get people to work at a high level of excellence and enthusiasm, try this on for size: work *for profit*. If work is a dirty word, profit has certainly acquired a most unpleasant odor. General Eisenhower said, some years ago, that "Profit has become a dirty word in Washington and dividends is even dirtier."

If profit is not a dirty word, then why does the State of Ohio put a full page ad in *The Wall Street Journal* saying: "Profit is not a dirty word in Ohio"? If profit is not a dirty word in Ohio, it must be somewhere.

David Lawrence, in an article in *U.S. News and World Report* entitled "Blessed Are the Work-Makers," said: "We hear profits lambasted as something sinful and management is pilloried as hard-hearted . . . we need neither 'black power' nor 'white power' but we do need brain power to build up profits. This is the way not only to increase the buying power of the people, but to add substantially to tax receipts."

Burnham P. Spann, former president of the Illinois State Chamber of Commerce and vice president of the Gardner-Denver Company in Quincy, Illinois, stated that "No major sector of our economic system is more maligned, less understood and surrounded by more false notions than is the role of profits." One of America's greatest labor statesmen once said, "The greatest crime a business can commit against its employees is to fail to make a profit. Companies without profits mean workers without jobs. Remember when the boss is in financial trouble, the worker's job isn't safe." That was Samuel Gompers. Some of his followers have strayed a long way from his philosophy.

From John W. Gardner, Secretary of Health, Education and Welfare in the Johnson administration, comes the following statement: "In the minds of some, leadership is associated with goals that are distasteful—power, profit, efficiency, and the like, but leadership, properly conceived, also serves the individual human goals that our society values so highly and we shall not achieve those goals without it."

A successful leader in any segment of our society must have economic acuity. This means that he comprehends the place and value of money, that he understands that he has to have more money than he spends or the institution that he heads will not continue to exist. It makes little difference whether the source of the money is payment for goods and services, taxes, or donations.

The American Management Associations has a very exciting program known as Operation Enterprise. This is a program in which high school and college students learn what management is from those who manage. In the course of the discussions, the question of whether one is in business to make money or to render services always arises.

It is soon brought out in discussion, and the young people usually discover it themselves, that making a profit is a service in itself. Virgil Martin, former president of Carson Pirie Scott in Chicago, has said: "A profitable company is a socially acceptable company."

In these discussions with the men at Operation Enterprise, we list the following services that profit renders:

1. Profit makes more and better goods and services available to the customer.
2. Profit makes more wages and benefits available to the worker.
3. Profit makes higher salaries and incentives available to the managers.
4. Profit makes more taxes available to government for the protection of our inalienable rights.

5. Profit makes essential community services available, such as churches, hospitals, libraries, museums, theaters, operas, symphonies, and so on.
6. Profit provides more money for research and development, thereby creating new products, more jobs, and increases the gross national income.

If money is, in itself, of value, if money makes more things of value available, it is important to understand that all money comes from profits. The challenge to management is to make every one of our followers believe this with a deep conviction.

Chapter 3

THE PROCESSES OF MANAGEMENT: *A* and *B*

The lawyer has formulas which guide him in his approach to a case; the doctor follows certain routines in diagnosing an illness; the mechanic has plans by which he inspects his machines; the engineer has definite rules that he follows regardless of what he is expecting to build. Therefore, it seems reasonable that a manager should have some simple processes which he can follow in approaching his job.

There is seldom much argument with the basic principles of management. The difficulty seems to lie in developing methods by which these principles may be applied easily. Out of an endeavor to solve that particular problem comes a conclusion which we believe leads to a very tangible and definite contribution to the field of management science. Following through on the earlier observation that management is a profession, we realize that members of other professions have processes for helping them solve their daily problems.

Professional processes are nothing but a series of steps which have been outlined and arranged in a logical sequence by predecessors in the profession. It tells those who are now in the profession that if they will follow those steps, they can rest assured that they have observed the basic principles of the profession and that necessary factors have been taken into consideration.

A problem in most organizations today is not to find new things to do, but how to do what is already known to be right. *If we can find a way to put to greater use that which we already know and have, we will have accomplished a great deal.* A professional approach should assist toward that end.

Management's job is to get people to work well and willingly. A management that can do that is good management. Any management that cannot do that is bad management.

The management process is motivating in itself. When special motivation programs and devices are required, it proves that the management process is not working correctly.

It is necessary at this point to make it clear that there is no attempt in this approach to reduce dealing with people to a pattern. Human relations cannot be reduced to a pattern, but you can have an orderly approach to human relations problems.

The processes themselves are a result of asking experienced and successful executives, over a period of nearly half a century, what, from their experience, they considered to be the most valuable advice they could give to their successors. These executives have been engaged in all kinds of organizations and businesses in some twenty-six different countries. The number and names of the processes have varied over the years but, basically, they remain about the same and continue to appear as the suggestions of successful management people.

The methods by which the processes are applied differ considerably and change often. They have brought about a common vocabulary, however, for terms of management and have established a basis upon which methods may be discussed. They also furnish a clarification under which the history and research of management can be coordinated and recorded.

It is important to remember that the greatest value to be derived from the application of the management processes is not the finished work, but the exchange necessary to securing the finished work. The discussions involved bring widely divergent viewpoints to a more common understanding. Workers better understand the motives and objectives of their supervisors. Supervisors gain a closer insight into the personalities and thinking of their managers. All of this is valuable. The more you direct minds into the same thought channels, the more reasonably sure you may be of accomplishing the objectives of your operations.

A management process puts into the hands of anyone in an executive or supervisory position a series of moves that he must make in order to secure the most desirable action. *It is a method of management.* It is a means of approaching any problem facing an individual who must supervise the activities of others.

Every process is now being applied in some way and to some extent by everyone in a managerial job. All this particular arrangement does is to bring these activities together in a simple, logical sequence that acts as a guide which, if followed, insures better attention to the steps involved. It is perfectly logical that the contents should not be new because of the nature of their origin. After all, it is simply an expression by successful executives as to the manner in which they work.

Management Process A: Determine Where We Are Now (Inventory)

Before being able to lead others in the attainment of a common objective, we must know where we are now. What are our strengths? What are our weaknesses? What are our assets? What are our liabilities?

The first step a new football coach takes is to make an inventory of what he has: How many men are there on the squad? How many of them are veterans? What kind of records did they individually have before coming to this team? Under what systems and coaches did they play? What is their individual speed? Their individual weight? Their intellectual capacity?

What kind of record does the particular team now to be coached have? What kind of conference or league is it in? What is the competition? What physical resources are available for practice and for games? What money is available?

Whether you are running a football team, a business, a church, a school, or a labor union, it seems reasonable that you should have an accurate knowledge of what you have before you can determine what you need and how to close the gap between the two. If young lovers would take such an inventory before marriage, they might change their plans as to time and place—and possibly as to individuals involved. Adults may admire the courage of youth, but they should remember that the young sometimes pay a high price for their rashness.

A most rewarding experience is to take an inventory of yourself. What are you? What do you believe? What is your philosophy? What are your guidelines? Economic status is extremely important. Physical and mental makeup have a direct bearing on one's future. Past accomplishments are important to determine trends and directions.

A few years ago I participated in the first week of an eight-month management program for graduate students. That first week was spent by the students in taking an inventory of themselves. One of the requirements was a statement of one's individual philosophy.

In the group was a fine looking, all-American athlete from one of our leading academic institutions. He had graduated with honors. He had an M.B.A. with honors from one of our most prestigious business schools. I watched him sit for over an hour with his legs stretched out in front of him under the table and the back of his head cradled in his hands as he stared at the ceiling. Finally I sat down next to him and said, "Tim, what's bothering you?" His answer was, "I feel just like a compost pile. I have been well fertilized but nothing has been planted."

The exercise of taking an inventory is both worthwhile and revealing. It is the basis from which management of one's self or leadership of others starts. Before we can set objectives and make plans for the future, we have to know whether we can "start from here."

Management Process *B*: Determine What We Want People to Do (Planning)

Every employee on the payroll should know what the overall plan of the company is and what particular contribution he is supposed to make toward its attainment.

In the summer of 1968 *Life* magazine ran an article entitled "Montgomery on Rommel" in which Montgomery told about the planning and preparations for the battle of Alamein. "My staff entirely approved and worked enthusiastically on the plan. . . . One further important point. I was determined that every officer and soldier in the Eighth Army should know the plan for the battle and his part in it. This was done on a careful plan, senior officers first and then down the several grades to the men in the ranks. The latter were told the day before the battle began, after which, no patrols were sent out; I would not risk losing any prisoners to the enemy at this stage. I reckon the men in the ranks of the Eighth Army knew more about the plan of the battle they were to fight than any other soldiers in history engaged in a major conflict."

34

A classic story that illustrated the value of knowledge of plans is that of the laborer digging holes. After Joe had been digging in one hole for some time, the foreman told him to climb out and dig one in another place. After Joe had dug to quite some depth in the new hole, the foreman took a look at it, shook his head negatively, and told Joe to start in somewhere else. When this procedure had been repeated four or five times, Joe threw down his shovel and said, with great feeling, "Dig a hole here, dig a hole there—dig, dig, dig! For what? I quit!" The foreman looked at him in astonishment and said, "Why, Joe, what's the matter with you? I'm trying to find a leak in a pipeline!" Joe's face lighted up. He picked up his shovel and went back to work with the comment, "That's different. I help."

Another story is told of the typical New York sidewalk superintendent who graces the fences where excavations are being made. This particular individual, while draped over a barrier, noticed two men with picks and shovels. They were both doing the same work. The observer asked the first what he was doing. The reply was one that might be expected: "I am digging a hole, what do you think?" He turned to the other fellow and asked him the same question, to which the reply was, "I am helping to build the foundation for a forty-story office building." Here was a difference in viewpoints, a difference in attitudes.

One of the greatest single influences upon worker attitude is knowledge of objectives—knowledge of what superiors are trying to accomplish—knowledge of the finished product, regardless of what small part the individual may play in its creation.

According to Ralph C. Davis, planning is "Determining what should be done, how it should be done, where action should be taken, who should be responsible for it, and why." The importance of planning cannot be overemphasized. It is seldom that anything can be accomplished any more exactly than it exists in the minds of men. It is one of the basic skills which makes management dynamic—it is the determination of what a manager wants to happen, and other skills are necessary to make it happen.

Planning is a mental clarification process. The best planning takes place when participation by all involved is secured. The best is that which comes from the bottom up in an organization. By the bottom we mean the lowest level of the organization affected by the planning.

Complete planning requires arriving at basic principles, long-range and short-range objectives, adequate procedure for the attainment of the objectives, and proper assignment of responsibility. Planning seems to be best when it is reduced to writing. Having to put something in writing seems to increase clarity of thinking and also facilitates communication of the plans to others.

Sometimes there is confusion between planning and policy formulation. There are those who maintain they are synonymous, and there are those who believe that one is part of the other. The main issue seems to relate to how extensive a policy is. Most people seem to think that policy is merely a statement of principles and objectives. To those who believe that, the major function of policy is to influence attitude, set tone, and control the climate in which plans are carried out.

POLICIES

With the possible exception of policies governing activities which are exclusively carried out by the board of directors and which guide certain of its decisions not put into effect by other members of the organization, policies should be put in writing. They are principles and objectives as well as statements of conditions which the management wants to exist and which lower echelons of management have to bring about.

There should be written policies on every major activity of the business. Effective decentralization depends upon the clarity of policy limits that have been established and within which authority can be delegated.

FORMAL PROGRAMS

A formal program is a written statement of needs, objectives, procedures, and assignment of responsibility. A program is formal when it is a conscious one, is known to be in existence, can be identified and measured. While it usually includes objectives, it is the outline of attack for the attainment of the objectives.

Programs should reflect the very best thinking of those involved in how certain tasks should be undertaken. They should be the result of complete participation by those who have to put them into effect. For every policy there is in the company, there should be a program—and undoubtedly there will be more programs than there are policies.

BUDGETS

A budget is a specific plan. It is an objective. Budgets reflect forecasting and policy making, and they become the standards for certain controls.

Budgets are distinct administrative tools. Every manager should have that segment of the budget which he is expected to control. This helps him to know what his contribution is to the overall budget, and he should understand the relationship that exists.

The most common practice, in relation to budgets, is for the department head, division manager, or plant superintendent to try to gain approval of a budget which contains higher expenses than he thinks he will need and lower income than he thinks he will produce. The reason for this is that he can then beat the budget by wide margins as a result of spending much less than the budget calls for and of earning far more. It is common belief that that is a commendable result.

That, however, is a vicious practice. A budget is supposed to be the course that a manager is going to follow and he should be watching it every day and every week. The minute results deviate from the budget, he must know why. If there is an indication of certain unexpected conditions, he must draw the attention of higher management to these conditions and, if necessary, propose a revision in the budget.

There are many managements that operate on a fixed budget and after it is once set, they never change it, regardless of what may happen. Normally, however, when they do that, they provide for operating estimates which project from month to month how far off the budget results are going to be. Others use flexible budgeting, which means that the budget changes every month and a new one is set up for the next twelve months. They are always working twelve months ahead.

The point being made here is that a budget is a tool of the manager and he must be acquainted with it and direct the efforts of his people in accordance with it. It is not an instrument which should be built, maintained, and carefully guarded by the financial department. It sets the course; and how can you know where to go if you do not know what the course is?

There are different kinds of budgets—financial, manufacturing, sales, and others. Usually, all of them ultimately key into one master budget which is the overall guide for top management.

AN IMPORTANT AND BASIC PRINCIPLE

In applying management techniques, it is imperative that we keep the techniques in proper perspective. No manager should develop any fondness for a technique in itself. I do not know of any manager who is devoting much time to the collection of *plans* just for the sake of having a collection of good plans. (Librarians and researchers, yes, but not managers.) I do not know of a manager interested in collecting position descriptions for the sake of having position descriptions.

Managers should not be interested in the development of perfect standards of performance just for the sake of attaining perfection in that medium. What *is* important is the process of applying the technique—the process of bringing a supervisor and a subordinate closer and closer together in their mental images of what is to be done and how well it is to be done.

The value of the use of a management technique is the impact it has upon human performance. This is the prime reason why it is important that managers use these techniques in working with their people, rather than having the techniques applied by experts.

Chapter 4

THE PROCESSES OF
MANAGEMENT: C

According to Lyndall F. Urwick, organizing is the management skill required for "dividing up all the activities which are necessary to any purpose and arranging them in groups which may be assigned to individuals." It is determining proper work assignments and relationships involved between people in the performance of their tasks. Its purpose is to so arrange group effort that the group can attain far more effective results under the type of organization structure used than under any other type.

Having determined the conditions which you believe will face the organization in the future, and having made the necessary plans to meet with success under these conditions, you next turn to the problem of organization. It takes a great deal of skill to determine what kind of organization will function most effectively under the circumstances that have been forecasted. Selecting the best type of organization requires time, effort, and thought. It cannot be left to chance.

Management Process C: Determine the People Needed to Do It (Organize Human Resources)

The term "organization clarification" means that anyone who has supervision over others should make sure that those people understand:

1. What their functions are.
2. What authority goes with those functions.
3. What relationships they have with others.

The activities that must be performed should be carefully and clearly determined. These activities should be divided into organization units and individual positions. Every person in the organization will then know what he is required to do, the extent to which he is to do it, and when he is expected to do it. The activities of each person will be related to each major activity, and individual work can be evaluated according to the contribution it makes to the accomplishment of the major objectives.

Clarification of functions, authority, and relationships is essential to good judgment because such clarification insures proper and complete consideration of the people and the factors involved in a problem. One of the great difficulties in organization is that either the wrong people are consulted or not enough people are consulted in arriving at a decision. There are those who, by intuition, sense the proper people and the proper factors to bring to bear on a given problem, but, unfortunately, there are not enough such people to go around in an expanding economy.

One of the problems faced in organization clarification work is delegation of authority. There are many reasons for caution and in some cases need for extreme reservation in the delegation of authority.

Because of the danger involved, there are few organizations in which a full or adequate amount of authority has been delegated. In every organization there are complaints about lack of authority. Executives and supervisors who have considered this problem extensively have come to the conclusion that the reason for this is a lack of knowledge of *how* to delegate authority.

Authority can be delegated adequately when two conditions exist:

1. When there is a definitely established policy within the limits of which authority can be delegated.
2. When there is recognition for proper use of authority and a penalty for misuse of it.

Authority can be delegated only within certain limits. Limits have to be established by policy. If there is no price policy, there can be no delegation of authority on price, but, if there is a price policy that has established a definite minimum price and a maximum price, then authority to change price within those limits can be delegated. If there is no salary policy, there can be no delegation of authority on salaries without serious consequence, but, if there is a policy establishing maximums and minimums for every job, and general principles to be followed in changing salaries within those limits, then authority can be delegated on that basis.

One of the common errors made is that when authority is delegated and misused, authority is taken away from the one who misused it, given to someone else as an extra load, and the individual who misused it is left in the same job with the same income. When authority is delegated, there should be frequent checking to see that it has not been misused.

In trying to determine what authority can be delegated, first make sure that there is a definite policy within the limits of which such delegation can be made, and then, after it is made, provide certain checks and balances for the purpose of reward or penalty.

There is a very simple and helpful device for clarifying

authority. After each function, include a (1), (2), (3), or (4). These symbols indicate the following authorities for the functions:

(1) Act.
(2) Act and tell.
(3) Act after consultation.
(4) Act upon instructions from another.

Activity Analysis

An interesting approach to organization clarification is that of the Activity Analysis. This method analyzes an activity through all positions and departments involved. It is clean-cut, definite, simple, and usable. *It does not replace the position description; it sometimes precedes it.*

The Activity Analysis has striking advantages over the traditional type of position description as an approach to organization clarification:

1. It catches all duplications.
2. It checks omissions of responsibility.
3. As soon as one activity has been completely analyzed, it can be put into effect as set up. It is not necessary to wait for the analyses of other activities.
4. It is fast, direct, and to the point.
5. It provides complete coordination of all jobs and departments involved. The Activity Analysis in final form is of practical use to everyone dealing with the activity.
6. Activity Analyses are a source of constant reference after they have been written. Proof of this is the number of revisions that take place as time goes on..

Making an activity analysis. Experience has taught us that the best Activity Analyses are made in group discussion.

43

Experience further discloses that a chalkboard is essential to this work. As thoughts are developed and crystallized on the board, the entire group has something upon which to concentrate. Changes are made and recorded; progress is definite and rapid.

CREATIVE DISCUSSION LEADERSHIP

Some years ago two college professors stated in a book they had written that there is no such thing as group creativity. They provided what they considered to be evidence that no group ever created anything that any single member of it could not have created. I frankly do not believe this. I have seen group creativity work frequently, over a period of forty years, in many different parts of the world with several nationalities and types of people.

There is a skill and a technique to group discussion leadership that results in group creativity. I have seen few masters of it.* Creative discussion leadership requires poise, confidence, and ability before a group. It requires the capacity to listen to what people say and to understand what they say. It requires the ability to reproduce what they say on the chalkboard—which, as noted above, is an absolute essential for creative group discussion.

---

*One of the greatest is Charles W. L. Foreman, a top officer of United Parcel Service, and a long-time participant, leader, teacher, and official in the American Management Associations. For many years he and I practiced it together and experimented extensively.

Two other men who come to mind are Dr. J. T. Marshman, former head of the Speech Department of Ohio Wesleyan University, and Dr. Elmer W. Smith, former head of the English Department at Colgate University, within which came speech training, including debate. Under Dr. Marshman I majored in speech and debated on the Ohio Wesleyan Varsity. Under Dr. Smith I taught speech and coached Varsity debate. In my opinion no training that I had contributed so much to whatever success I have had in my career as my experience in speech with Drs. Marshman and Smith.

44

In group discussion, the thought of one person creates a thought in the mind of another. This process goes on and on in an atmosphere of creativity. Thought is stimulated and ideas result from such stimulation. The end result is the product of the group and the group is committed to it unless some individual violently objects, and that is most unusual in the successful exercise of such a process.

The most simple guide to one who wants to use creative group discussion is this: make sure you have clearly in mind the problem or subject to be discussed; have the very best answer you yourself can think up before the discussion starts; do not tell anybody else what your solution is; get a better solution or answer from the group than you had at the beginning. When this happens, the group has contributed to your thinking. You know it, and they know it. They belong to what has been produced.

A Sense of Belonging. One of the most effective ways to give people a realization of "belongingness" is to ask them to help you as their leader: take an inventory of where the group is; determine where the group should go; determine who and what is needed to get the group there; determine how well individuals in the group should perform; determine how well they are performing; determine what is needed to help them perform better; and determine how they should share in the outcome. This works! I know it works! But let me remind you it takes a deep belief in human values and skill in conducting group discussions.

This is the time in civilization when a desire to belong is stronger than it ever has been. Successful leadership requires that we respond accordingly.

Steps in Conducting the Discussion. The first step in creative group discussion is for the leader of the group to identify and put on the chalkboard the problem or subject for discussion. Order is unimportant. You can start with any activity mentioned. Usually the group will designate an activity that is causing trouble or that is particularly pertinent

45

at that moment. Such a situation adds to the interest and value of the work.

Before going any further, the leader must have the agreement of the group that that is the problem or subject and that it is worded correctly. The leader then asks someone for a solution to the problem or for a statement in relation to the subject. This he writes on the chalkboard. (Creative group discussion requires a great deal of chalkboard plus "flip-flop" crayon pads.) If it is not clear what the person wants written on the board, the leader stays with it until it is clear to the suggester as well as the group.

What is originally on the board will be added to, subtracted from, altered, and may end up as something completely different from what was originally written. The discussion group is concentrating on what is being developed because it is on the board in front of them. Frequently it is written on the large sheets of the flip-flop pad, and these are torn off from time to time and put up on the walls around the discussion room with magnetic tape. This records the progress of the discussion.

When nothing more is to be contributed and what is on the chalkboard is agreeable to the group and represents a consensus, it is then taken down by a stenographer, typed, duplicated, and passed out to the members of the group very soon after that problem or subject has been concluded. The members then see what they have created, and I have yet to meet a member who has participated in such a process who hasn't admitted that the end result of the group process was different from what he had in mind when the discussion started.

Suppose, for example, that the group has selected budgets as the activity to be analyzed. There are different kinds of budgets. They would have to select the particular budget they want discussed. Assume that they select a budget for capital expenditures. That would become a heading which would have to be broken down into its various elements.

46

At this point the chalkboard would have an outline that looks something like this:

ACTIVITY
Budgets
Capital Expenditures
  Preparation of
  Administration of
  Appropriations
  Requisitions

Some groups will develop an extensive outline of activities to be discussed. Others will start with the first activity mentioned.

When the group is ready to analyze the first activity selected, the next item to consider is the position with which the action on that activity originates. Having determined that, you then write after that position an exact statement of responsibility. This responsibility can be in the form of a single verb, a phrase, a sentence, or a paragraph.

ACTIVITY	POSITIONS INVOLVED	RESPONSIBILITY
Budgets		
Capital Expenditures		
Preparation of:	1. Salesman	Survey his territory; determine needs; by Oct. 1st submit recommendations on Form B-493 to ———.
	2. ———	

A flow of *responsibility* has been started. It is necessary to determine the position to which the activity next proceeds. For illustration, let us say it is the Field Office Budget Clerk. That title is written in after "2. ———" above. The responsibility of that position is then fixed. The work on the chalkboard now looks something like this:

ACTIVITY	POSITIONS INVOLVED	RESPONSIBILITY
Budgets Capital Expenditures Preparation of:	1. Salesman	Survey his territory; determine needs; by Oct. 1st submit recommendations on Form B-493 to ———.
	2. Field Office Budget Clerk	Check existing leases and purchase options; correlate all recommendations into District recommendations; submit with comments by Oct. 15 to ———.
	3. District Manager	

The verbs are extremely important. Words such as "survey," "check," "correlate," "submit," "review," "endorse," "authorize," and "approve" all have distinctly different meanings. All indicate basic relationships. All show different degrees of authority. Verbs should be clearly defined so that their meanings and limitations are well understood by the whole organization.

It is necessary to remember, and it is a great cause of confusion if we do not, that the purpose is to *fix responsibility* and to *indicate flow of responsibility,* and to write detailed methods. In other words, the Activity Analysis should show *what* is to be done, *when* it is to be done, and *who* is to do it; but not *how* it is to be done.

You then continue on through to the ultimate conclusion of the procedure. As soon as an activity has been completed and meets with the approval of the group or of the chief, the person acting as secretary copies it. It is later typed, duplicated, and issued.

There are certain liberties that can be taken with an Activity Analysis if certain rules governing interpretations have been established. These rules are usually agreed to by the groups concerned and appear at the beginning of organization manuals containing Activity Analyses. Establishment of such interpretative items eliminates the necessity of repeating certain words or phrases in every analysis. Such items as outlined by one organization are as follows:

1. *The procedure outlined in each Activity Analysis is flexible.* While the procedure is written as an ideal way to handle each activity, and while the order suggested seems logical, actual handling of the activity might not necessarily follow the order written. The important feature to remember is that all of the steps listed should be taken before a final decision is reached.

2. Most of the procedures are written as progressing from one point in the organization to another. If the problem involved always originated with position No. 1, the flow would proceed to the highest numbered position. *A recommendation, however, may originate at any one of the positions along the line.* When this occurs, the procedure is to go back to position No. 1 and then up, so that all those involved are fully acquainted with what is going on and opportunities for contributions are given to all before the final authority deals with the problem. Recognition of this rule eliminates the necessity of incorporating the word "initiate" after many positions in the procedure.

3. In some cases an analysis follows through to the point of approval and stops. In other cases it goes from the point of approval on through other positions, or possibly back to the source. *When a procedure does not show what happens after approval,* notification goes back through the same channel through which the subject came.

4. Words indicating positive action, such as approve and endorse, imply the right of *negative* action, such as disapprove. If this is not understood as a general rule, then it is necessary every time you write "approve" to write "approve or disapprove." It is also understood that when negative action

actually takes place, the subject is referred back through the channels by which it came, rather than on up.

5. The right of appeal is accepted as existing in any organization. While this is not indicated in any procedure, it is understood that any time a recommendation is rejected, an individual always has the right to take the recommendation to a higher authority with the knowledge of the individual who rejected it. In other words, if a division staff member refuses to endorse action recommended by a district manager, the district manager can appeal to the division manager with the knowledge of the staff member involved. Very often such appeal is made jointly.

6. Where more than one title appears after a number it is interpreted as the same step in the procedure, and all the positions in that group are contacted by the position shown in the preceding number. The statement of responsibility appearing after this group of titles applies to all of them unless otherwise indicated.

7. Wherever a title appears without a qualifying word in front of it, such as "division" or "district," it always refers to a headquarters position. For example, if the procedure reads "Marketing Assistant, Research," it is a headquarters position. "Division Marketing Assistant, Research" is quickly identified as a division position.

8. Sometimes general terms are used to indicate bodies, such as "Management," "Division Management," "Executive Committee," and so on. When such general terms are used, they should be clearly understood. The general term should stand for a regularly constituted body.

9. In many places where a position title should appear, you may find "Staff Member Involved." In such cases it should be easy to determine what staff member is involved because of the nature of the subject. *Staff members so indicated include both staff and line positions.* For example, they could include the head of a products department, which is a staff

position, as well as the operations manager, which is a line position but a part of the general manager's staff.

PREPARATION FOR ACTIVITY ANALYSIS DISCUSSIONS

Aside from an agenda, little preparation for these discussions is required. There will always be someone who will conscientiously prepare an Activity Analysis on his own subjects for presentation to the group. Experience so far has shown that analyses so prepared seldom remain intact. There is usually disagreement and revision of the very first step, which leads to a different second step, and from that point on the previously prepared procedure is discarded.

Sometimes there is a feeling that certain procedures do not justify the time of the entire group and should be prepared by committees or departments, endorsed by the group, and placed in the manual. That was suggested in a conference of the United States Civil Service Commission, and this was the reaction: "It was decided to proceed with the regular analysis every meeting so as to make progress with the charting of activities not yet considered. A suggestion by Mr. ———— that the Budget and Planning Division prepare tentative charts of activities not yet considered in order to save time of the . . . Conference was rejected on the ground that this would be depriving the members of the Conference of an opportunity to familiarize themselves with techniques and procedures with which they should become familiar."

Some individuals like to prepare lists of subjects pertaining to their own activities. While this is not necessary, it has met with some success, and those who do it, like it. The statement that it is not necessary grows from the experience that each discussion brings out several activities to be clarified in future discussions. This list is continually growing and is always ahead of the group.

There are various media used for the preparation of lists

51

of subjects. The simplest is just a scratch pad on the desk on which are listed the subjects which are dealt with day after day over a period of three or four weeks. This list may include subjects of interviews, correspondence, telephone calls, telegrams, cables, meetings, and so on. Certain individuals have their file clerks or secretaries pick subjects from the file, while others even use a file index.

THE VALUE OF USING EXACT POSITION TITLES

A conscientious attempt should be made to use specific titles in the Activity Analyses. A practice sometimes creeps into the work which is not particularly desirable. That is the practice of showing that an activity flows from a position to a division or department. When the title of the department is used, the inference is that the activity flows to the head of that department, whereas in many instances this is not the case.

One of the values of the Activity Analysis is the reduction and elimination of red tape. If it is possible for an activity to flow from some position well down in one department or branch directly to a position well down in another department or branch, without passing through the executive heads of those organizations, that should be encouraged as much as possible.

Tradition has established a desire to acknowledge rank, which sometimes creates a tremendous amount of delay and handling. In many organizations there is a tradition that rank writes to rank, or in other words, a division manager should write to a division manager. In many cases all that is involved is that the other division manager immediately refers it to one of his clerks without looking at it. In many instances the second division manager never sees it because his secretary or assistant takes it out of his mail and sends it to the proper point.

If the activity does not require the attention of a particular position, there is no reason for pertinent correspondence or contacts to pass through that position. If properly set up, the Activity Analysis will protect prestige and rank and will eliminate many steps that have been previously considered necessary.

FINAL DISPOSITION OF ACTIVITY ANALYSES

When a discussion group writes an analysis, usual practice is for the secretary to copy the final form from the blackboard, make it up in duplicate copies, and issue these copies to the members of the group before the next session. When the next session convenes, the analysis is reviewed and approved. The secretary then makes copies of the final draft and sends them to the members to be included in a folder for that purpose. This becomes a part of what ultimately will be the Organization Manual.

One of the common difficulties encountered is the revision of procedures previously written. The best work and thought are put into the first draft. From there on, changes are very detailed in nature and involve changing words or their arrangement. If a group should write an Activity Analysis and then review it for the next twenty sessions, changes would be made with every review. It seems sound practice, therefore, to establish a rule that a procedure is written in one session, reviewed at the beginning of the next one, and then issued. Any further revisions should come as a result of use rather than because of a conscientious attempt to revise.

Regimentation?

Organization clarification necessarily means defining the areas in which people work. Some believe this means regimentation. We may as well face that objection and face it squarely. When a plea is made in defense of individual liberty and initiative, it is necessary to point out that an individual who joins an organization must immediately accept certain restrictions that he would not be required to accept were he on his own. Instead of doing what he pleases, when he pleases, and where he pleases, he now must direct his efforts within certain channels. If there are desired activities which organization restrictions do not permit him to perform, he must await his opportunity through transfer or through proper enlargement in the scope of his work.

When individuals are allowed to follow their own instincts in an organization, their performance becomes unbalanced. They do what they most want to do and what their particular capacities fit them to do, and they devote their entire efforts to these fields. Other responsibilities which good organization demands on the job are neglected. This causes failure in the overall result or necessitates the assumption of these responsibilities by others.

When talking about organization clarification, it is essential to recognize what Chester I. Barnard has so ably described in his book *The Functions of the Executive*. He refers to the informal phase of organization which is never clarified or codified. It exists in any organization regardless of how much clarification takes place. It can best be illustrated by stating that if an executive were walking down the hall of an office building and saw a fire in somebody's wastebasket, he would not go by and do nothing about it simply because his position description did not list fire fighting as one of his responsibilities. He would rise to the occasion and do what was required. Therefore, even though we have formal descriptions of what should be clarified, we must leave room for common sense and judgment in relation to things which have not been formalized.

Clarification Needed in Every Organization

The need for outlining responsibilities, authority, and relationships exists not only in business and industry; it exists wherever you find human beings, regardless of the type of organization.

Does it not seem perfectly reasonable and logical that any individual in any organization should know what he is supposed to do, how much authority he has, and what his relationships are with other people? Does it not seem obvious that to the extent such knowledge does not exist, you will find duplication of effort, omission of responsibility, friction, jealousy, politics, and all the forces that defeat the very purpose of organization?

Such clarification cannot be brought about by wishful thinking or high-sounding philosophies. It takes hard, careful, well-organized, continuous effort. It means analyzing an activity from its inception to its conclusion through jobs and departments. It means developing a flow of work indicating who does what, when, and to what extent.

Organization structure is the control which makes it possible for individuals to work together in groups as effectively as they would work alone. That is why we have organization structure. There is no other purpose for it. It is very interesting, in attacking individual problem cases involving morale or personal relationships, to trace the organization structure concerned. You usually will find that the difficulty arises from misunderstanding or confusion as to individual responsibility, authority, and relationships with other people. If an organization structure is not sound, the people in it cannot perform properly. Successful administration requires simple, understandable organization structure.

These principles and observations seem so fundamentally sound that they are presented with some finality. Therefore, it is necessary to repeat that these are not the convictions of any one individual, but of many individuals with great experience and breadth of view.

An organization is an extension of the chief executive. He delegates what he wants, as he wants, and to whom he wants. While he has an ideal organization structure toward which all personnel moves should be made, he has a current structure that must be adapted to the competency of the help available and the degree of confidence he has in that help. Organization structure should be constantly changing and a subject of continuing study.

The Catholic Church is famous for its skill in organizing. Its full-time workers are educated and trained in the structure. Military establishments are highly organized and their officers and troops are on the receiving end of considerable training and review of organization structure. You can say the same about athletics. Why, then, do we neglect organization clarification in other segments of our society?

If we were still using the flying wedge as the best football formation, there would not be much interest in football. Along came outstanding coaches, however, who introduced the single wing, the double wing, the T formation, the I formation, the lonely end, the blitzkrieg, the shotgun, and the wishbone. Alert coaches are developing new formations and they sometimes use several during a game.

Coaches cannot do this without spending hours and days in chalk talks with the players. The players have to know the organization structure and the part each plays in it. Let each manager search his own soul. How much time have you spent in the last twelve months discussing organization structure with your team? How in the world can you expect it to operate as a team if you do not work at it? Team play doesn't just happen.

Because most of us have learned organization structure from our military experience, we are trying to inflict military organization upon civilian activities and it doesn't work very well. Any manager who copies an organization structure out of a book is not fulfilling his professional responsibility.

One of the greatest deterrents to human effectiveness is the attempt to apply military organization structure to civilian activities. They are completely different human situations.

Military organization is created for split-second timing. The infantry, artillery, engineers, communications, supplies must all be at a certain place at a certain time. Judgment is rarely required and is never asked for unless something goes wrong and headquarters cannot be contacted. It is quite the opposite in civilian institutions. Managers are paid primarily for the judgment they must exercise. While timing is important, it is not paramount.

The military offers the highest motivation that any human being could have: love of one's country. This motivation may make a person willing to lay down his or her life for his or her country. Such motivation is rarely present in civilian institutions. This makes a big difference. Since the process of leadership is within itself the greatest motivation, the process must be different when the motivation required is greater.

Military organization, furthermore, has the court martial to support it. This is a very convenient device. Nothing like it exists in civilian institutions. Is there any wonder that we have made such a catastrophe of civilian organization structure because of our blind adherence to our limited organization knowledge—military?

The Chain of Command

Establishing the chain of command calls for the determination of authority and also the levels of authority. In its simplest form, it is answering the basic question, "Who is the boss?" While individuals can work with and serve many people, it is not fair to ask them to be responsible to more than one person. Some individual has to have the authority to determine the responsibilities, authority, effectiveness, and rewards of another individual.

The levels of authority and command vary by types of organizations and situations. The main principle involved is that the number of levels should be kept at an absolute minimum. Not only should the number of levels be kept at a minimum, but also a constant attempt has to be made to keep final authority as far down in the chain of command as possible. Organizations should be permitted to make final decisions just as near the point of operation as possible.

A territorial salesman for an oil company discovered a desirable piece of land near Portland, Maine, which he felt would be an excellent site for a service station. He followed the book in making up his recommendations—made a market and traffic survey, discovered the availability and price of the land, estimated cost of investment and of operation, figured out what the realization could be over a five-year period, secured photographs, real estate charts, and so on. All this was submitted in proper form to the district manager. The district manager, real estate manager, sales manager, and others all went out to see the property. They added what they were supposed to add to the recommendation and sent it to the division office.

Out of the division office came the real estate man, the sales manager, the engineer, and others, and they looked over the property, added their recommendations, and sent them on to headquarters. No one in the headquarters' office for the eastern territory bothered to go to Maine, but the recommendation went across the desks of twelve different executives. From there, it went to the marketing headquarters for the entire company. A similar process was followed. Finally it reached the board of directors. The board approved it and back down through all the levels it went.

When it reached the salesman in Portland, Maine, some fourteen months later, the salesman wrote across it, "The XYZ oil company has purchased the property and has been operating a profitable station on it for the last four months." That was the end of that! It led to a complete reexamination of how to speed up important decisions of this kind.

It is in the establishment of the chain of command that we become involved in the problem of centralization versus decentralization. Decentralization can be in terms of authority, as well as geographic. It takes a lot of skill, persistence, intestinal fortitude, and faith to push responsibility down the chain of command and keep it there.

One of the primary difficulties in decentralization is the lack of appreciation that real decentralization must take place with centralized control. That means that responsibility and authority are delegated within the limits of established policy. This in turn implies that decentralization can take place only when planning and policy formulation have been effective.

Span of Control

The span of control is the number of individuals who can be supervised effectively by one person. It answers the question as to how many immediate subordinates a manager should have.

There have been many dogmatic rules established in relation to span of control. There are those who say that no individual can control the activities of more than six or seven people. There are others who say it is ten or twelve. Most of the argument that takes place is in relation to the number of individuals that can be controlled rather than with the principle that a span of control should be established.

Basically the answer depends on the organization and the skills of the executive involved. The answer to it is found when you can determine for how many subordinates a manager can: skillfully plan their work; assign their work; organize them; establish standards of performance for what they are to accomplish; review their performance; and take constructive action for reducing their weaknesses, capitalizing on their strengths, and getting greater and greater production from their efforts. This all has to be interpreted in terms of the existing morale.

One of the greatest tragedies in management is when

the members of the staff of an executive cannot see him because he is too busy with "more important matters." The first and primary responsibility is to work with the people who look to him for leadership. If they require more of his time than he thinks justified, then he had better question their capabilities. If, on the other hand, they cannot get as much time from him as they deserve, then he had better question his own capabilities.

The skill to establish the proper span of control is a very specific one and its application requires conscious and determined effort.

A Challenge

The greatest asset of any nation is the productivity of its workforce. Nothing has any value until human effort makes it so. Gold, silver, diamonds, oil have no value in the ground. Human effort has to get these resources out of the ground, make them usable, and get them to those who wish to use them. Charles DeGaulle found this out during the general strike which he had to settle before the franc lost all its value.

The purpose of any organization is to get certain work done effectively. This requires getting people to produce certain desired results. The purpose of an organization structure is to get people to produce results more effectively in a group than they can produce alone.

There is no type of organization structure in existence today anywhere that does not interfere with, rather than enhance, individual productivity—civilian or military. All are outmoded and obsolete. Evidence of this is the anti-establishment sentiment that is prevalent today in civilian life, and the fact that we can't win wars anymore with our military structure. There has not been a new organization concept in this century. There has been almost complete failure to recognize differences between individuals and changes in all individuals.

Brand new creative thinking in depth is required. In order to attain greater productivity, management people must become more competent and exact in the determination of the work to be done and they must attain greater knowledge of how to motivate people to do it. There must be far greater skills in both areas: work clarification and human motivation.

We must discover new mechanisms for improving relationships between people at work—mechanisms that enhance their output. For example, there should be greater use of peer pressure as compared with the line of command. The old master–servant, boss–subordinate relationship is no longer acceptable. The human being is evolving from a being to a human. Modern "bosses" are not trained or able to obtain today's needed products and services from today's humans. The universal failures of church, school, government, and business are proof of this.

The great challenge of the moment for management is to find ways and means to develop knowledge and skills in work clarification, work standards, and motivation. We have talked about it, written about it, and even prayed over it. It is now time to face up to the task at hand and to what has to be done to develop the kinds of human relationships that result in productive effort. Productivity is the name of the game!

Chapter 5

THE PROCESSES OF MANAGEMENT: *D* and *E*

In order to operate, an organization needs office and plant facilities, equipment, money, and materials. The ability to know what is required, and when and how to secure it, is a skill.

Management Process *D*: Determine What the People Need to Do It (Organize Physical Resources)

The initial acquisition of the physical needs of an organization is one problem. Additions and replacements are another problem. One has to sense potential growth and needs and has to attune them very carefully to plans.

It takes a lot of courage to withdraw money from the bank or borrow it to provide adequate facilities for the accomplishment of dreams. That, however, is one of the things for which management is paid. It is one of the risks an individual takes. If he suddenly finds his organization enjoying a growth and demand for services for which he had planned and hoped, but finds he cannot meet that demand because of inadequate physical facilities, he is in a tragic situation. On the other hand, if he provides plant and equipment which ultimate demand does not justify, he is in just as serious a predicament.

That is why determining physical resources is identified as a skill. That is why planning and organizing are important bulwarks for judgment in relation to facilities. To this has to be added faith in one's own leadership and in that of one's staff. The reason for identifying it here, however, is to emphasize again that the specific skills required by management have to be burned into one's consciousness and require continuous attention and development.

Management Process *E*: Determine How Well People Should Do It (Standards of Performance)

Standards of performance are statements of conditions that will exist when a job is well done. Each person contributing to the desired result within an organization should have the same understanding of it as all others within the organization.

Can you imagine what would happen in the football stadium or the baseball park if no agreement existed among the members of the team as to the results they were trying to secure? Can you imagine the coach sending the star halfback out on the field with instructions to take the ball and run and keep running, paying no attention to the goal line, the stadium, or anything else, run anywhere, run as fast as he can, never stop running? No, the coach does not do that. He tells his backfield to get the ball and make a first down on three tries (not four, because usually you have to kick on the fourth down). That constitutes satisfactory performance. *That is the standard.* If, by chance, the ball carrier can make a touchdown on one try, then he produces better than satisfactory performance and will be recognized for it.

63

While the coach is enthusiastic over super-performance, he will, at the same time, be perfectly satisfied if the standard is reached.

Managers, supervisors, and foremen should have definite objectives for the activities which they are supervising. They should know what constitutes a job well done. They should reduce to writing for each activity, or group of activities, statements of conditions that will result if the work is done as it should be done. It is a pleasant surprise, when starting to work out standards, to see the tremendous improvements that immediately take place. The reason is a better and a more common understanding of objectives.

A great experience awaits the executive or supervisor who calls together his immediate subordinates for a conference to develop standards of performance. In answer to the first question, "What are the major activities of the job that should be measured?" he will be amazed at the difference in opinions and at the length of time it takes to get agreement.

When an executive then selects one of these activities and asks the question, "What are the conditions that will exist if this factor of the job is well done?" he will be startled at the great variation in answers. People responsible for the same activities, people doing the same work, people who are supposed to be getting the same result, will have as many different opinions when asked that question as there are people to utter them. It is quite a thrill to see minds finally come together in common agreement upon simple, definite statements.

Does it not seem reasonable that individuals working toward a common objective should have uniform concepts and agreement as to that objective? Does it not seem reasonable that they will work together better as a group and will accomplish more as individuals? Again, standards are not developed by wishful thinking or by high-sounding philosophies. Patient, continuous, well-organized effort is required to produce the type of standards that will create the attitudes and produce the performance desired.

Writing a complete set of standards for a job or group of jobs establishes job balance. It gives proper evaluation to the various phases of the job. It also focuses attention upon dimensions of the job that would otherwise be unnoticed.

It is a fairly well accepted principle that it is good to commend people for work well done. It is all the more effective when such commendation can be given at the time the work is done. This is an extremely important morale builder. There are practical difficulties, however, which prevent commendation being given as frequently as it should be, or even at the time it should be.

When an individual has standards of performance, he *knows* what constitutes a job well done. At the end of each day, he knows whether he has done what is expected of him or whether he has exceeded it. Even though his superior may not know it at the time or be anywhere near him—not being able, therefore, to commend him—*he* has the satisfaction of knowing how he stands. He knows that ultimately the record will show a satisfactory performance. In the absence of personal commendation, therefore, such realization is, in itself, a morale builder. Standards of performance have a very important function in that regard, as well as the other advantages which can be attributed to them.

The most commonly known standards of performance are those which are engineered. They are used for production jobs where exact measurements of time, motion, and cost can be made. Industrial engineers are well trained in setting standards. They are experts with well over seventy years of experience behind them. Most companies have them in some form. In other words, they are used for accurately measurable output and are guided in their establishment by people who know their business.

Non-engineered standards are a different matter. The approach to them should be just as scientific and just as careful, but most of the standards are not as exact or measurable. Standards can be established for any job in terms of quantity, quality, cost, and time even though the meeting of standards is frequently a matter of judgment rather than exact measurement.

Because of the inexactness of non-engineered standards and because they have to be set primarily by people doing the work for which standards are being set rather than by experts, there has not been much progress in this area of management. There is a steadily increasing interest in the subject, however; and for that reason, we will go into considerable detail in describing how non-engineered standards can be set.

Keeping in mind the principle of consultative supervision, we find that the approach to the development of standards of performance is that of group discussion. Those who are expected to reach certain levels of performance should contribute to the development of what those levels are.

When should standards of performance be developed? Should we wait until the organization clarification work has been completed, or can we start on standards while jobs are being clarified, or can we start standards without any clarification of jobs? Experience so far dictates no rule in this respect. All three have proved successful. The main variable seems to be the time required. If responsibility has been clarified in relation to an activity before a standard has been written for that activity, less time is required to write the standard. The reverse of this is true: if a standard has been written, it takes less time to clarify the activity.

Some groups will clarify an entire activity, placing responsibility and developing relationships on an Activity Analysis basis, and will then write a standard of performance with its respective subdivisions before moving on to the analysis of another activity. Sometimes only a general standard is written rather than a specific one. Practice varies, however, and the results always seem to be about the same. The guiding principle here is to let the group decide which procedure is to be followed.

MAJOR SEGMENTS OF PERFORMANCE

A position naturally divides itself into the major activities with which it deals. Such division takes place during either the organization clarification or the standards of performance work, whichever is done first. Whether it is review of what has been done during organization clarification or an initial approach to the entire question, the first objective of the group is to list on the chalkboard the major segment of the job, giving to each part the name of an activity.

Suppose for example that a group of salesmen are in conference for the purpose of developing standards of performance. The first question asked by the discussion leader is, "What are the major activities of the job in which performance is reflected?" The group will then develop a list that may look something like this:

> Sales volume.
> Controllable selling expense.
> Realization.
> Credit and collections.
> Attention to market conditions.
> Application of product knowledge.
> Work organization.
> Condition at reseller outlets.
> Attitude of customers.
> Attitude of public.
> Contributions to company policy.
> Routine details.

The wording of a few of the foregoing items is rather interesting, such as "attention to market conditions" and "application of product knowledge." This wording is the result of very careful consideration by sales groups. They observe that it isn't the amount of product knowledge a man has that is important, it is what he does with his knowledge. It is not the actual market conditions that are important in relation to a salesman's performance, it is what he does about those conditions. This accounts for the words "attention to" appearing in front of "market conditions" and "application of" appearing in front of "product knowledge."

The development of the list may take an hour; it may take half a day. Regardless of the length of time, it is a most important development. As soon as it is completed each salesman in the group has a new concept of his job. He sees his responsibility in more complete and more balanced form. It is quite possible that he previously thought of his job as 90 percent sales volume and 10 percent annoying details relating to sales results. He now sees that there are twelve major parts to his job, all of which require attention.

While a salesman's job is used here as an illustration, the same procedure is followed for any job. Whereas the list of major segments will be different for different jobs, the effect upon the conference group is the same.

A STANDARD OF PERFORMANCE

Having developed a list of the major segments of performance, the discussion leader would now ask the group to select one of those segments for which to develop standards. Usually the group will select the first one on the list, although the order is not important. Assume for the sake of example that sales volume is selected.

The major segment "Sales Volume" is now placed at the top of the chalkboard and under it an introductory statement which assists the sequence of thought and also clarifies the group's objective.

This is a most interesting experience. Here is a group of salesmen varying from those with little experience to those with long experience. There will be healthy, lengthy, and illuminating arguments about which items are to be included as standards and the wording of each item. A salesman will

I. *Sales Volume*

Satisfactory performance has been attained by the salesman in relation to sales volume when the following conditions exist in his area:

1. ———
2. ———
3. ———

Etc., etc.

suggest the first statement to be put down. It may not even get on the board before another salesman has changed a word, a phrase, or the whole idea. However, the discussion continues until a statement appears as Item No. 1 which is acceptable to all. The discussion leader will then ask for another standard, and another, until the group feels that all of the standards that should be listed in relation to sales volume are now on the board. The discussion has probably developed something like this:

I. *Sales Volume*

Satisfactory performance has been attained by the salesman when the following conditions exist in his area:

1. Quotas for all products have been attained or exceeded. (See Monthly Quota Sheet No. 608.)
2. Ratios of branded vs. unbranded products have been maintained as follows:

   Branded greases to all greases, etc.:———%
   Branded motor oils to all motor oils:———%
   Regular gasoline to special gasoline:———%
3. Etc., etc.

Standards of performance are now in the making. Having completed the first major factor selected, which is sales volume, we then ask for the next factor to be discussed. It may be "Controllable Selling Expense." The same procedure is followed until standards have been written for all the major factors of performance.

Measurable vs. immeasurable standards. In this development of standards of performance the objective is to use those standards which can be measured definitely by facts or figures. Theoretically it should be possible to determine beyond all question that a certain standard has been reached, not reached, or exceeded by the employee. While this may be a desirable objective, it is not always attainable.

Because of this objective on standards, the group applies the test "Is that standard measurable?" The question will be raised repeatedly in the course of the discussion. Many times when the answer is no the group will fight to retain the standard because it is of value and should be a continuing subject of discussion.

Noble and practical as the measurable standard may be, a requirement to attain it in all cases seems undesirable. After all, standards of performance should reflect the aspects of an employee's daily activities that ought to be topics of discussion between the employee and his supervisor at the time of the progress review. Employee groups will usually concede that a certain amount of individual judgment is required by their manager. They realize that executive judgment is one of the qualities for which a company pays. Therefore they are willing to leave certain standards which do not appear to be supportable by facts and figures to the judgment of the supervisor as to whether they have attained. Of course, such judgment is arrived at in consultation with the employee.

Use of standards brings improvement. Many individuals who have not participated in a group discussion during which standards have been developed become quite critical when they see those that have been written. They pick many imperfections in the subject material and in the wording of these standards. It is important to remember that the first standards written, poor as they may be, are better than anything that existed previously. Better standards will be written only after the first ones have been used.

One improvement in standards, evolving with usage, is the reduction in the *number* of standards. The group members soon realize with experience that it is better to direct their efforts toward the attainment of a few standards, all of which can be covered in discussions with their immediate supervisor, than it is to have a large number, many of which are neglected both in effort and in discussion. Another improvement will be noticed in the wording, and still another in the compactness of the standards themselves.

Statistics required to support standards. After considerable discussion, a basic fact suddenly becomes apparent: standards of performance should deal with the basic results that management desires and which are actually secured through individual performance. Any manager should have statistics available to tell him the progress he is making toward the accomplishment of basic results. If standards, therefore, properly reflect the results desired and present statistics are not set up to indicate the accomplishments in relation to these objectives, then perhaps it is not additional statistics we need but rather revision of existing statistics.

People who are responsible for making reports and records are constantly begging units of the organization to tell them what is wanted. Because of the indefiniteness of the answers, the statistical people must often use their own judgment and set up figures as best they can. This very careful, detailed study of standards of performance provides statistical people with the answers for which they have been pleading. It tells them what the executive needs to know. If they will consider the standards in that light, they will welcome them and will find from experience that the ultimate requirement is fewer but more usable statistics.

Time required for development of standards. The time required for the development of standards is an essential consideration. More time should be allotted for the first attempt than for the subsequent sessions. This is because it takes time to get the hang of it. Unless very carefully handled, suspicion on the part of the employees involved is usually a first reaction since standards sound a bit like efficiency.

It takes time to get employees to the point where they are willing to talk, to express themselves freely and honestly. They have a fear that their reactions are a bit ludicrous because they rightfully expect that there must be more definite objectives in someone's mind. As the discussion progresses and they find that the reactions coming out are no more definite than their own, they gain confidence and soon take an active part in the discussion.

One of the greatest benefits of this work on standards of performance is not the finished material that goes on the chalkboard but the discussion that takes place in getting it there. Managers obtain unexpected reactions from employees, ability is discovered that was not known to exist, and employees gain a conception and understanding of their supervisors' thinking that they never had before. It is a process of discovery. It is inspirational, invigorating, and challenging.

After each session held, immediate results are noticeable. The attention of employees is directed to items of performance that they never knew about or had forgotten. Time consumed in such discussions is more than recovered by greater productiveness or by better use of time on the job.

Types of positions for which standards can be developed. It is important to point out that most of the technical development of work standards has been for definite production jobs, particularly in manufacturing plants. Time and motion studies have been made of physical improvement required to perform a certain task. Where that kind of job exists, the engineered standard takes the place of what is being suggested here. The major purpose of this step is to apply that same kind of approach to general jobs that cannot be so specifically measured, and to the general aspects of specific production jobs.

It is no longer difficult to measure the productiveness of a worker on the assembly line. It *is* difficult to measure the productiveness of white collar workers in the office. A few years ago it was considered impossible to measure the overall productiveness of such jobs as selling, engineering, and supervision. It is to this latter classification that the discussion just covered applies.

Experience shows that standards of performance can be written for any job. The more definite the job, the more definite and measurable the standards. The more general the job, the greater the results from the development of standards.

The plea here is that regardless of the job, an attempt should be made to write standards of performance for it. Each attempt will produce better standards; all attempts will produce better attitudes and better results. Imperfect and immeasurable as they may be, they are still better than none.

Standards for standards of performance. If standards of performance are properly written, certain conditions in relation to those standards will exist. In order to get the greatest benefit from the development and use of standards, standards of performance should be:

1. Jointly developed by employees and their supervisor.
2. Statements of basic results required of the operation.
3. Worded to include references to accurate means of measurement.
4. Worded to prevent multiple interpretations or misinterpretations.
5. Measurements of quantity and/or quality of work performed.
6. Set up in officially approved form.
7. Attainable by at least one member of the group concerned.
8. Continually revised with use.

Standards of performance in relation to organization clarification. The organization clarification work provides us with Activity Analyses indicating flow of responsibility through all positions and departments, as well as with position descriptions. A natural question arises as to whether standards are written for activities and/or for jobs. If so, should there be a standard of performance for each activity and/or for each function of a job?

The general answer is, first, that standards of performance can be written for activities and/or for jobs, but that there are fewer standards than there are activities or functions of a job. Common practice is to write general standards for major divisions of activities and specific standards for positions dealing with these activities.

For example, an Activity Analysis might be divided into twenty-one major divisions, such as sales, expense, realization, personnel, operations, accounting, statistics, engineering, and so forth. For each of these, a general overall objective would be prepared, which is often called an objective rather than a standard. This is then broken down into specific and more detailed standards for each of the positions involved in these activities. Each job would have detailed standards for only that number of the twenty-one major divisions with which it deals. Whereas the marketing department might have its activities divided into twenty-one major sections, the sales and engineering departments might be involved in only twelve of them.

There might be forty-six functions of a specific job. Using these functions as a reference only, sixteen standards of performance might result. The reason for this is two-fold. In the first place, one standard might cover five or six functions. In the second place, there may be some functions for which no standard can be written but which have to be performed if the overall written objective is to be obtained.

It often comes out in the discussions that there are a number of functions an employee is expected to perform for which there are no standards of performance or no possible methods of measurement. The function is either performed or it is not performed, and measurement must depend upon the integrity and industry of the employee. Do not, however, place functions in this classification too quickly. Submit them first to a very careful analysis.

Chapter 6

THE PROCESSES OF
MANAGEMENT: *F*

People in positions of supervision should periodically compare
the present performance of individuals under their direction
with the standards of performance that have been established.
This requires the ability to tell people exactly what you think
of their performance and still command their respect and
confidence.

Management Process *F*: Determine How Well
They Do It (Progress Review)

This is a most difficult aspect of supervision. It is the point
at which managers and supervisors analyze the performance
of their organizations as compared with the objectives. The
work of the processes up to this point—clarification of jobs,
setting of standards—is preparation for this step. All that
follows is based upon the findings of this step.

This is the point at which "problem cases" must be faced

squarely. Many individuals are known to be problems by everyone in the organization except themselves. Attempts are made to transfer our "problems" to other departments by misrepresenting their qualifications and their performance. Management cannot and dare not evade individual problem cases. Neither can it transfer those problems nor eliminate them until every possible effort has been made to solve each problem by dealing with it on an individual and understanding basis. It is interesting to note that leaders who have the capacity to discuss the performance of individuals with those individuals themselves, and at the same time create mutual confidence and respect, have few so-called "problem cases" in their organizations.

CURRENT VS. PERIODIC COMPLETE CHECKING

When periodic checking of complete performance is advocated, this reaction is often expressed: "We're continually checking performance. As irregularities come to the attention of the supervisor, he immediately discusses them with the employee involved." Such a comment requires clarification of periodic and complete checking versus current checking as needs indicate. Both are important. One without the other is not always sufficient. Current checking, however, always has been done and is being done. The contribution that a progress review makes is a complete performance review at definite intervals so that the employee may see his own balance sheet. Continual check-up and careful supervision will always be required. The development of a periodic balanced picture is the purpose of Process F.

A discussion between supervisor and employee at time of failure is not always sound. Such a discussion may be subject to the emotions of the moment, and when emotions enter, reason exists. A husband may at some time, for reasons beyond his control, find himself the bridge partner of his wife. He may make some unpardonable error. Comment by his wife at that time is not only discourteous, but may reflect bitterness and may include unreasonable observations. If she would wait until some other time, her instruction would be much more beneficial and social gossips would not have material with which to spread the "confidential" information of a home split by strife and conflict.

Another value of periodic progress review is that it provides an opportunity for commendation, as well as condemnation. This seems to be a sound, psychological principle. It is not conducive to good morale to "bawl out" an individual for poor performance without also conveying to the individual an expressed hope of improvement or an expression of pleasure for some success he has had. When going over the employee's performance in its entirety, both good and bad performance are discussed, and some failure which might seem serious by itself may be insignificant as compared with a number of indicated successes.

Good performance and morale require, and are immediately responsive to, a close relationship between man and boss: confidence of one in the other's frank, open, inspirational leadership. A tremendous power in any organization is the feeling on the part of the worker, "I like to work for that man."

Good performance cannot be secured by remote control, by executive order, or by written instructions. It does not exist simply because we think it exists. It will exist only when worker and supervisor are working closely together, and when their thoughts are running in similar channels.

If the executive or supervisory function is to determine what has to be done, to discover how well it is being done, and to develop methods of bringing actual accomplishment closer to objectives, then this is the point at which actual performance is discovered. How else can it be done but to check individual performance against objectives?

At an AMA meeting some years ago this definition was worked out: "Appraisal is the development of accurate under-

standings on the part of responsible executives of the qualifications and needs of individuals and groups of individuals to
meet organizational requirements." Since the skill to appraise
covers both individuals and operations, it would appear that
this definition is not inclusive enough. This calls for the presentation of a particular viewpoint which, in my opinion,
makes the following definition all-inclusive: *The most comprehensive and effective review and appraisal of operations
is that which is done through the appraisal of those people
who perform the operations.* The two should not be separated.

Unfortunately, statistical records of operating results have
been commonly considered as quite a separate process from
"ratings" of human beings. This differentiation has not been
a good one. It is a result of failure to put sufficient emphasis
upon performance when making human appraisals.

The primary reason for appraising an individual should
be to evaluate his performance and discover ways and means
by which he can develop so as to improve his performance.
Consideration of personal qualities and of potential should
be based upon a sound appraisal of performance.

If an individual has organized properly the activities of
people under his immediate supervision, and if he has delegated adequately the responsibilities which should be delegated to these individuals, then an appraisal of their performance will give him the most complete review of what is
happening in the operations for which he is responsible. Every
phase of his responsibilities will come under the microscope.

When an executive reviews and appraises the performance of one member of his staff, he is looking at one complete
segment of the operations for which he is responsible; he
is determining how they are being handled by the person
in charge; and he is deciding what action should be taken.
They are all closely interrelated. The only corrective action
that can be taken must be taken through individuals.

There is no more valuable or critical judgment required
than that called for in the appraisal of a human being. It

seems reasonable to assume that if the judgment of many is of value in arriving at decisions in relation to physical resources, the same should apply to human resources. The judgment of one person about the effectiveness of another is not as good as the judgment of several. Greater skill can be acquired, therefore, when an executive asks others to help him in appraising the competency of his own people.

It was Thomas A. Edison, I believe, who said, "Forty heads are better than one." This is an extreme, of course, when we are talking about appraising, but, if forty heads are better than one, then four heads must be better than one, and that is the principle to which we are referring.

Progress review is a basic management skill requiring a lot of conscious attention, practice, time, and effort. The benefits resulting therefrom, however, are probably among the greatest of those enjoyed from improvement in any of the skills of management.

Rating systems are not new. They have been in use for a long time and there are many of them. A large percentage of managements use them. There are all kinds and types. Personally, I do not care for the word "rating" nor do I like the implication of it. It implies classifying an individual in relation to other individuals and is based upon a grade which is expressed in figures, percentage points, letters, or simple terms such as satisfactory, average, poor. Please do not interpret this to mean that I personally am not in favor of such systems. What I am trying to say is that I do not believe they are adequate in themselves.

The main purpose of an appraisal of an individual should be to discover what can be done to improve him and to help him develop to his greatest potential. It is constructive in nature. What we are primarily interested in is how his performance compares with the standard for the job and how his potential stacks up in relation to bigger jobs. We then want to improve his performance and give his potential full opportunity to develop.

Appraisal of human beings, therefore, should be primarily the responsibility of their immediate supervisor. Appraisals should be made by the boss, kept by the boss, and used by the boss. Staff assistance is extremely valuable and, in many cases, absolutely essential, but the concept that appraisals are being made for a staff department and for somebody's files must be religiously and consciously avoided.

CONFERENCE, GROUP, OR MULTIPLE APPRAISALS

The conference, group, or multiple appraisal is rapidly coming into popularity. The theory behind it is that while the immediate boss is responsible for making the appraisal, he can do a better job with the help of others; that a group of people appraising another in a discussion will get a fairer and more accurate result than if individuals do the appraising separately or if one appraises and another concurs or rejects it.

The question is frequently asked, "What about prejudice and dominating personalities in such appraisal discussions?" The answer to this is that people are much more careful and accurate in their appraisals of others when they are held accountable for such appraisals than when they are not. Human beings are much more cautious, fair, and reasonable when what they say about others becomes a recorded judgment, which management has asked for, than they are in loose, irresponsible conversation. One of the great tragedies of human nature is what we say about other people when it does not have to be supported.

One of the reasons appraising is so difficult is that we are poorly prepared for it. When an immediate supervisor has taken the time to arrive at an appraisal of one of his subordinates in a discussion with other responsible people, he is better prepared and is quite confident about the result.

The term "open appraisal" means that the result of the appraising is discussed with the appraised. People have been hesitant about this in the past because when they do the appraising alone, they find themselves frequently in arguments with an individual when discussing the appraisal with him. It is the boss against the man. When, however, he has had the assistance of others in making the appraisal, he becomes the representative of the appraisal group to the man appraised, as well as his representative to the group. If the appraisal is inaccurate, it is very easy for the boss to say that he will take the matter up with the appraisal group for reconsideration.

The form included on the following pages for illustrative purposes is in use by a number of companies. It is practically self-explanatory. Note that most of the emphasis is upon performance, which breaks down into both results and methods. This is because two people can attain the same results, but one can be using methods that will ruin the company or a department, while another is building future strength into it.

Note also that the personal qualifications listed are only those which are outstanding. No attempt is made to go through *all* qualifications. Just list those which come to mind when you think about the individual being appraised. If there is nothing outstanding about his mental facility, do not say anything about it. If he is above or below average, however, and noticeably so, it should be mentioned. If he has an unusual length and breadth of experience for his particular job, that should be mentioned. And so on.

Individuals doing appraising sometimes shy away from giving opinions as to potential. They will say they have no idea how far an individual can go or will go. Why should a manager shy away from this any more than he does from the budget, or from forecasting, or from what he thinks the output of a particular machine will be? All he is being asked for is his best judgment and he has just as much right to judgment about people as he has about money, materials, and machines. Strangely enough, judgment about people frequently is more accurate than about physical resources.

It is not necessary to discuss "potential" and "action to

PROGRESS REVIEW

NAME_____ POSITION_____ DATE_____

AGE_____ LENGTH OF SERVICE_____ YEARS ON PRESENT JOB_____
This Summary Appraisal is a narrative description developed from a detailed analysis of the employee's work.

PERFORMANCE

RESULTS (What has this individual accomplished in measurable results since his last appraisal? Consider quantity, quality, cost, and time element of work. Give facts and figures wherever possible. Consider human relationships. Be specific.)

_____
_____
_____
_____
_____
_____
_____
_____
_____
_____

METHODS (How does this person go about getting his job done? How does he work with and through people? Be specific.)

_____
_____
_____
_____
_____
_____
_____
_____
_____
_____
_____

PERSONAL QUALIFICATIONS

List only outstanding qualifications either above or below average.

GENERAL_____
_____
_____
_____
_____
_____

STRONGEST SINGLE QUALIFICATION_____
_____

OPPORTUNITIES FOR IMPROVEMENT_____

POTENTIAL

What is the next step ahead for this individual and does he have further potential beyond next step? If so, outline
_____
_____
_____

ACTION

☐ LEAVE ON PRESENT JOB_____

    (Recommend action for improvement such as training, change of attitude, change in pay, encouragement, etc.)
_____
_____
_____

    ☐ PUT ON PROBATION   UNTIL WHAT DATE?_____

    ☐ PROMOTE   ☐ DEMOTE TO_____

    ☐ TRANSFER TO JOB OF   ☐ TERMINATE

       SAME CLASSIFICATION

WHEN SHOULD RECOMMENDED ACTION BE TAKEN?_____

CURRENT STATUS

☐ IMMEDIATELY PROMOTABLE	☐ SATISFACTORY PLUS	☐ DECISION DEFERRED BECAUSE NEW	☐ UNSATISFACTORY
☐ PROMOTABLE	☐ SATISFACTORY	☐ QUESTIONABLE	☐ UNSATISFACTORY; ACTION DATE SET

APPRAISAL MADE BY

NAME_____   TITLE_____

NAME_____   TITLE_____

NAME_____   TITLE_____

NAME_____   TITLE_____

NAME_____   TITLE_____

The performance and personal qualification sections of this report have been discussed with the employee by,

NAME_____   TITLE_____   DATE_____

be taken" with the appraised. That does not mean you should not do so, but it does mean that there are many *situations* in which you should not do so. If it is the opinion of a group that some young man will some day have the capacity to be president of a company, you could quickly ruin him by telling him so. On the other hand, there might be some individual who has been appraised as never being able to do more than he is doing and yet he is doing his present job well. You might completely break his morale by telling him he has no greater potential—and you could be wrong. If you have decided, for some reason, to take a man off a job, the timing of telling him so must be carefully handled. For this reason it is not always advisable to tell him that at the time you discuss the appraisal with him.

Toward the bottom of the second side of the form is a series of phrases, one of which is to be checked for an overall key to the man. It indicates whether he is immediately promotable, ultimately promotable, satisfactory on the job, and so on. This is for use in the making of a personnel inventory chart. An inventory chart is simply an organization chart in code, either color code or variations of black and white. Quick reference to this chart tells you how your organization stacks up—where your strength is, where the weaknesses are, how deep your reserves are, and similar facts.

It is important that we state again that when a manager has made a conference appraisal of all of his key people, when he has discussed the appraisals with them, and when he is taking definite action to improve conditions that are not right, he has reviewed all the operations for which he is responsible and he is taking corrective action. This is the way in which he controls the performance of his team and in which he obtains the results he is after. It is a method of management.

In the course of conference appraisals, many things take place other than just the appraisal of an individual. Conditions are discovered which prove the inadequacy of policies, plans, and procedures. Something which has been consistently considered the fault of a man sometimes shows up to be the fault of the system or policy under which he is operating. Changes in organization relationships take place and sometimes changes in basic structure.

Use of the multiple, conference, or group appraisal is a wonderful experience. Rating systems, control statistics, progress reports, are all information used in conjunction with the conference appraisal work.

Many of us have toiled and worried over interpretation of results because statistics have not been adequate or the required information has not been available. If investigation were geared down to each and every employee, we would be much more comprehensive in our analysis and much more accurate in our decisions.

Reticence on the part of supervisors and executives to do this individual analysis work has been because of the lack of a proper approach to a very personal situation—the actual performance of a single worker. If functions have been clarified, if standards have been set, then a very simple and sound basis of discussion has been established. Such interviews become less complicated and far less awesome.

The question is frequently asked, "Why is there so little contact of this nature between man and boss; why does a manager so infrequently tell the people working for him exactly what he thinks of them in terms of their performance, their qualifications, and their potential?" One reason is that it is one of the most difficult functions to perform. If there is any question in one's mind as to the difficulty involved in criticizing another and still retaining his respect and confidence, a simple illustration may help.

The person who is the closest to a man—who knows him the best and whom he knows the best and with whom he has the most comfortable relationship—is his wife. If there is anyone with whom he should be able to discuss personal matters, it is she. Consider, if you will, the number of times you have returned home late at night from some place she did not want you to be, and what happened upon your arrival at home. Then, think of other times when, in the same situation, you thought to yourself on the way home, "This is the time I am going to tell her exactly what I think of her. I am not going to put up with past performance in such situations any longer." Count up the number of times you made such a resolution and then against that, put the number of times you actually did what you resolved to do—and then you know what is meant when it is said that it is the most difficult aspect of human relationships—to criticize another and still retain respect and confidence.

It is easier to do when the preparation for it has been thorough, when you have confidence that your findings are reasonably fair and accurate, and when you are supported in your opinions by other responsible people.

Chapter 7

THE PROCESSES OF MANAGEMENT: *G* and *H*

Having decided the functions of each job, having decided the results that will be secured if the job is well done, and having discovered how well each employee is performing as compared with the standards, an executive or supervisor has the required information to determine what each person under his direction requires for individual improvement. That seems to be the intelligent and commonsense basis for a training program.

It seems better to base our training courses and our instructional work on the individual needs of the people in the organization rather than upon some fine, costly program developed at headquarters which half the people in the organization do not want and few need. If management processes have been applied intelligently up to this point, enough individual and group needs will have been discovered for training programs to last the company for an indefinite period.

Management Process G: Determine What Help People Need to Do Better (Development and Controls)

This particular process provides each employee with a definite program of individual development so that he may perform more satisfactorily and willingly. He is conscious of the fact that his management is trying its best to improve him as an individual and to make him of greater value to society. This is where the real function of management comes to the front. A leader is measured by the extent to which he helps develop those under his direction. This is a morale builder if there ever was one, and better morale means greater productiveness.

FORMAL TRAINING

This presentation of processes of management might lead one to believe that formal training is relegated to an area of less importance. *Formal training is more important than it ever was.* It is based, however, on the needs for such training as indicated by careful, personal analyses.

Under the old method, there would be a staff of technical experts and editorial writers in a training department who would turn out material. It seems far more sound to refer such requests to the staff department that is dealing specifically with the activity involved. That department should have more information on the technical or professional subject than anyone else. The staff can prepare and edit material and, in fact, it is a basic organization principle that the staff department should provide the organization with adequate information about its own activity. If there is no staff department in connection with the activity involved, then some outside agency or specialist may be employed for the assignment.

First, be sure that the formal technical or professional courses are based on the actual needs of the organization;

second, that full use is made of the facilities in the organization; and third, that the very finest courses are ultimately developed and supplied.

Since formal training and special technical courses are practices of long standing in most organizations and have been developed to a high degree, it is not necessary to discuss them here. It is necessary, however, to emphasize that this is the point at which the need for formal training is determined with great care and completeness.

INFORMAL GUIDANCE

A great deal of development is advice and guidance as to what should be done to solve a particular problem or to meet a job situation. This may be a suggestion as to what an individual should do, or it may mean a change in policy, plan, or procedure. It may even take the form of changing responsibility assignment. While this is training of a nature, it is primarily arriving at the solution to something requiring immediate action.

The best formal training methods, conferences, and courses are built around the solution of practical problems anyhow. Much more comes out of progress review than just an inventory of a person. It usually results in a change in practice of some kind or in a change in the climate and conditions in which a person performs responsibilities.

Having determined what action is required as a result of the progress review, it is necessary to select the very best source from which to secure it. If the determination of what is needed has been accurate, the same sound judgment can be applied effectively to the selection of the proper persons or sources to meet the need.

Generally speaking, there are at least four sources of help. The first is the most important and the others should not be considered until the first has been eliminated. They are (1) the immediate supervisor, (2) a company specialist, (3) an outside source to be brought in, (4) an outside source to which to go.

The help needed may be for the purpose of changing attitudes. This may simply be a matter of contacting certain people or taking part in certain group discussions.

Possibly greater skill or additional knowledge is required. This is the point at which participation by staff specialists and department heads may be solicited. It is not uncommon that participation in field activities by a headquarters staff person is largely due to his own initiative. It is a much healthier condition when his field participation is increased due to invitations from the field.

There are specialists in certain subjects, outside the company, whose services may be secured. A very thorough investigation, however, should be conducted before any individual or group in the organization receives the help of a specialist. The specialist must be practical, likable, know his subject, and be able to present it well. In addition, he must be able to adapt himself and his material to the organization.

A very common practice in industry is that known as the educational refund plan. When employees are encouraged to attend outside institutions of learning, companies under such a plan pay a part or all of the cost.

The problem may be one of habit. The immediate supervisor is the best possible source of habit-changing efforts. Habits can be changed only through continual coaching, help, and guidance. This comes with daily supervision.

A definite point in time should be established for taking indicated action. If all the processes have been applied up to this point and definite time is not arranged for supplying what is needed, much may be lost. Here again, the importance of planning must be emphasized. Time does not become available. It must be *made* available. When specific periods are set aside for required training and development, the organization soon adjusts itself to the schedule.

The value of budgeting time should be obvious. Books

have been written about it; all kinds of schemes and gadgets have been worked out to assist in it. Still, we do not do enough of it. If time is planned in advance—and well in advance—many of the bridges we fear do not have to be crossed.

REGULARLY SCHEDULED MEETINGS

The question always arises as to meetings. "We already have too many meetings," someone remarks, "and now we are to have more meetings." It has been definitely proved that if meetings are regularly scheduled and everyone knows that on certain days each week, or each month, he is to attend a meeting, there are fewer meetings held than when they are called as needed.

Much of the unfavorable reaction to meetings arises from the practice of notifying people on Friday that they are to be at a meeting on Monday. Confusion is caused, changes in plans are necessary, vacations are interrupted, other people are inconvenienced, the work of the day piles up and is not done. The reaction on the part of the people in the meeting is not favorable. Many of them appear with files of correspondence or memos which must be answered. They occupy themselves with the contents of such material rather than participating in the discussion.

If a salesman, truck driver, clerk, supervisor, or executive knows well in advance that at a certain time he is expected to attend a meeting, he makes no other appointments for that time; he arranges his activities, he provides for the handling of his work, and there is little, if any, disruption of his activities.

TIME SCHEDULES FOR INDIVIDUALS OR GROUPS

When it becomes apparent in the course of a progress review with an employee that the help of some other employee is needed, pick up the telephone and make a date in advance.

If, in making progress reviews, needs are discovered to be common to an entire group, list the subject on the agenda for a future meeting.

The time schedule takes the form of individual appointments or dates for sessions of the entire group. Experience indicates that as a result of inventories, plans, organization clarification, standards of performance, and progress reviews, enough needs arise to justify the establishment of regular meetings for the group involved.

Regular meetings are set up on the basis of a certain day each month, or twice a month, or each week, depending on the nature of the group and the necessity for group consultation or group help. For example, the executive group meets on the third Thursday of each month. Each member of that group meets with his own supervisory staff on the fourth Wednesday of each month. They in turn meet with their supervisors and foremen on the second Tuesday of each month, until ultimately employee groups are reached, meeting on definite days at a specified time. The whole point involved is to set a time in advance for doing what your very careful analysis indicates ought to be done.

The common sense of such planning seems to be obvious and unquestioned. The difficulty is in training ourselves to do it. If conferences and individual interviews or individual training are planned, if there are agendas in advance, if the people are prepared, if the sessions themselves are carefully and objectively conducted, if careful minutes are kept, then each such session will pay dividends.

TIME FOR CONTACTS OUTSIDE THE COMPANY

It was not so long ago when anyone who suggested that a manager might spend weeks off the job for the purpose of receiving further education and training would have been classified as impractical, theoretical, and academic. He even might have been called a dreamer. Today, however, this is a widely recognized and confirmed practice. The number of executives who are attending professional conferences and seminars, where they are taking part in valuable exchange of experience and where they are keeping up to date on trends and problems, is increasing by the thousands.

Out of these contacts grow relationships through which individual executives visit companies for varying periods of time in order to find out how others deal with particular problems. Correspondence and telephones keep men up to date with their counterparts in other companies. All this adds up to one of the great dynamic characteristics of the kind of economy in which we live. Our willingness to exchange our know-how with others keeps the whole structure sound.

CONTROLS

We will not go into any elaborate discussion of the subject of controls here. We will simply identify a few so as to clarify what we mean by controls. All those mentioned are well known to every manager, and all that is needed is an exchange of experience on method.

Some of the controls available to a manager are: cost systems, financial statements, break-even charts, return on investment analyses, work measurement, internal auditing, cash forecasts, budgets, and many other statistics.

Alert management will have the tools it requires to watch carefully the relationships between expense and income; profits and capital invested, as well as sales; cash positions; quality of product and service and its maintenance; time and materials waste; the effectiveness of policies, plans, and procedures; reliability in the handling of assets and funds; the adequacy and reliability of information and statistics, and so forth. Not only does an alert management watch these things through the establishment of the finest controls, but it has an obligation to do so in order to keep the ownership adequately and honestly informed.

93

Again, this list of controls and the items to be controlled are not complete. They are presented for the purpose of illustration with the strong appeal that men in management know beyond any question of a doubt what controls are, what controls there are, and which they should use.

Management Process *H*: Determine What We Will Pay (Rewards and Incentives)

Incentives and rewards are both financial and nonfinancial. The question is frequently asked which are the more important. It is very difficult to answer that question, because it depends upon certain basic conditions. Until an individual has attained a level of financial return from his work which is reasonably well related to other jobs of similar value, to the standard of living which the company expects of incumbents, and to the basic economic necessities of the family which he is raising, financial incentives may be of greater value than nonfinancial. After he has reached that economic status, even though it may not be as liberal or high as he could wish for, his interests shift to the work climate in which he finds himself, to the kind of management and associates with whom he works, and to certain job satisfactions which arise from the kind of work he does and how he does it.

There are too many cases of individuals who have refused to take job offers in other companies, where the pay is higher, or who have left a company to join another for a job where the pay is lower, to underestimate the importance of nonfinancial considerations. At the same time, there have been many individuals who have had to make changes they did not want to make for no other reasons than economic necessity. Therefore it is difficult to generalize. Each case has to be considered in terms of the specific circumstances.

It is good to be able to report that top managements are giving more consideration to this problem than ever before

94

in history. There has been very full and ready participation in important surveys of executive compensation. Companies are more willing than ever before to exchange information of a very confidential nature in order to secure the benefits of such exchange.

The compensation pattern that has been left as a result of the upward squeeze of labor rates is not a good one. The differential between workers and first-line supervisors has been radically decreased. White collar workers and middle management people have been caught in an unsatisfactory situation. On top of all this is the decreasing return for high-income executives resulting from the tax burden.

What is important to remember is that if an organization is to be kept high in morale, high in productivity, and competitive in a free economy, rewards and incentives must be kept adequate to encourage that "job plus" for which America is so famous.

JOB ANALYSIS AND EVALUATION

Job analysis and job evaluation are common tools of management. They have been used for a number of years and are basic to any intelligent reward and incentive program. Job analysis is simply analyzing the job in terms of its duties, its responsibilities, its scope, its authority, the experience and training required, the skills required, and so on. We enter job evaluation when we give to each of the factors of the job analysis a weighted value. When jobs have been analyzed and weightings have been given to the various major factors of the job, then the different jobs are compared.

By this means, it is possible to compare a janitor's job with that of a president; a mechanic with a salesman; a clerk with an engineer. Jobs are then put into groupings which may run from one to ten or one to sixteen, as the case may be. These groupings include the positions which have equivalent weightings.

Following this, income surveys are made within the community to find out what the prevailing rates are for similar jobs. Income surveys are another illustration of the amazing development in American management. Salaries and wages, as recently as thirty years ago, were confidential, "sacred" information. Companies are now exchanging this information quite freely.

When prevailing rates have been discovered for similar jobs, money values are placed on each of the job groupings in the job evaluation. Maximums and minimums are listed and then the bases for increases within the limits are set.

It is most encouraging to see the extent to which job analysis and job evaluation are moving from lower levels up into higher levels of management. Company job evaluation programs now include everyone through the presidency.

Bonuses, stock option plans, profit sharing are all incentive tools. Rather than go into detailed discussion on this here, our only objective is to identify what we are talking about and to urge that managements give careful attention to their reward and incentive programs. Organizations are more sensitive to the soundness and fairness of compensation than to any other single factor.

The length of discussion so far on financial rewards and incentives might lead one to believe that we regard them as more important than nonfinancial incentives. That, however, is not so. The nonfinancial incentives are most important after a certain minimum standard has been attained on the financial ones. To put the idea in extreme terms, it would be possible for the nonfinancial incentives to be so great in a company that an employee would love to work for that company for nothing—if that were possible. He has to live and eat, however, and support a family. There are certain financial rewards, therefore, that are an absolute necessity for him. After that minimum has been attained, then the nonfinancial incentives become important.

These nonfinancial incentives are the management climate, the type of associates with whom he works, the general working conditions, and the human satisfactions of work. Probably the greatest nonfinancial incentive for a manager is to be able to come to the end of a year with the realization that the people who work for him are better workers and better citizens because he was their boss. It is a great thrill to be able to look at your team and to realize that *you* put it together, that *you* trained it, that *you* put morale and fight into it; and that it is accomplishing results which would not be accomplished if *you* were not the leader.

It is good for any management to appreciate its financial rewards and incentives to make sure that they are fair, adequate, progressive, and as good as they can be in the light of company capacity to pay. The management should then clearly list and identify the nonfinancial incentives and be just as conscientious in their efforts to make them what they ought to be.

Chapter 8

THE CHARACTER IN
MANAGEMENT

One of the great gratifications in my life is active participation in Operation Enterprise of the American Management Associations. This is a dialogue between actual and prospective leaders concerning the meaning of management and its basic processes. From time to time, these young people have small group sessions to determine questions they would like to ask of mature leaders. Some time ago, one of these questions read as follows: "What are the differences between a mediocre manager and an enlightened leader?" Older leaders were embarrassed not to have an immediate answer.

The question, however, was challenging and since that time there have been many discussions of the subject. While the answer is still evolving, its development up to this point is profoundly interesting. In brief form, it is as follows:

Assuming that both the mediocre manager and the inspired leader have the basic requirements that any manager would have to have to remain on the payroll—honesty, in-

y, technical capability, loyalty—there are at least five
characteristics that separate excellence from mediocrity.
1. *The inspired leader has a record of attainment.* He
accomplished something which society and/or his asso-
s attribute to his unquestioned leadership.

2. *He has a mission.* He has a purpose in life that is
d at helping other people rather than exploiting them.
is motivated by something other than "the almighty dol-
If he is manufacturing shoes, he is manufacturing a par-
lar quality at a particular price, for a particular kind of
ple who otherwise might not have such shoes. If he is
ting insurance policies, he is doing it in order to give
viduals a type of security they otherwise would not have.
le is a doctor, his prime interest is in keeping his patients
l and he is not an ambulance chaser. If he is a lawyer,
concern is for justice, and he will not take every case
that comes into the office regardless of its merit. If he is
a teacher, he uses the subject matter as a means of reaching
the life and the character of the student. His—or her—devotion
to a cause, like his drive and dynamism, is sparked by purpose,
by mission!

3. *The inspired leader practices consultative supervision.*
Some call it participative management. It means that the
leader deeply believes that his organization is full of creativity,
of talent, of knowledge, of ideas, of helpfulness. He believes
that he is on the receiving end of a fantastic source of information rather than being himself the source of all knowledge.
He is humbled by this.

It is extremely interesting to me that the trends of the
times are making consultative supervision an absolute necessity. Absolute, dictatorial, conceited management is outmoded. A belief on the part of the boss that he possesses
the greatest brain and finest judgment is obsolete. Such beliefs
are as old and unacceptable as Hitler and Mussolini.

One of the greatest modern writers, who died in 1972,
was Dr. Abraham H. Maslow, a behavioral scientist. I first

99

came to know about him and his works back in the early 1950s from Dr. Douglas McGregor, president of Antioch and later a member of the faculty of the Massachusetts Institute of Technology. Maslow set forth his "hierarchy of human needs" in his book *Motivation and Personality,* published in 1954.

This hierarchy has at its base or first step "survival." This is a physiological need for air, water, food, shelter, and so on. The next step up is the human need for "safety and security." The third step up the ladder is for "love and belongingness," while the fourth is for "esteem" (by self and by others). At the top we find "self-actualization." The last is a need for individuality, perfection, justice, order, meaningfulness, and so forth.

It is my humble belief that the signs of the times, the current pressures by individuals and by society, the drives for recognition by minorities, the expressions aganst the establishment, and other developments of this nature are indicators that civilization, at least in the United States of America, finds itself at the middle level of this hierarchy of human needs—"love and belongingness."

In my travels about the world, dealing with younger and older adults in practically all the major areas of our society, I believe I sense more than anything else *the desire to belong,* to be a part of and to participate in something worthwhile, and to be recognized for it.

In Chapter 9, one of the skills of management is described as "instilling the service motive." A story is told of war workers in a radar plant (p. 114). No one even bothered to tell them of the importance of their work, menial as it might have been. In my opinion, and in my experience, there is no work so menial, so dirty, so routine, so unpleasant that it cannot be made desirable to the worker if he is made to believe that he and his work contribute to the attainment of something that is worthwhile.

Many managers today employ able management consultants to come into their organizations and secure information from their people, put it in a book, and sell it to the management—even though it was available to the management for the asking. Even on this basis, it is the inclination of many leaders to bury such a consultant's report in a desk and do nothing about it.

It is a lonely life a manager leads when the knowledge and ideas of other people are of no interest to him. It is reasonable to assume that his leadership life is also shorter.

4. *The inspired leader is intellectually mature.* This means that he has basic, deep convictions in relation to those issues having an important impact upon his life. It means he is willing to stand up and be counted. He is ready and willing to participate in the affairs of the community of which he is a part, not on the basis of some pious obligation, but on the basis of a strong desire to support his convictions. It means that the leader recognizes that he must have an impact upon his environment and his environment is nothing but a bundle of issues. He must be straightened out in his own mind in relation to these and know the direction he will take. His influence must be continually felt because of the strength and the sincerity of his beliefs. This, however, is just half of it. Intellectual maturity is not only a matter of convictions; it is also the ability to change convictions when new truths indicate such change is appropriate.

5. *The inspired leader is emotionally stable.* There are few, or minor, conflicts between his basic beliefs, his convictions, his philosophy, and the way in which he lives. If his day-to-day activites require him to do what his conscience tells him he should not do, he has an appropriate degree of emotional instability. If the two are mildly incompatible, he has a neurosis. If they are profoundly so, he may require psychiatric treatment. One cannot continue, if he is intellectually mature, to live a life that is contrary to one's basic makeup without suffering thereby.

Leaders and potential leaders can be trained, can be

educated, to make things happen: so that they can identify, clarify, and follow a mission; so that they can benefit from the knowledge and experience of other people; so that they will have up-to-the-minute beliefs and convictions supported and tested by a continuing knowledge of current developments; so that they can live with their consciences and can face themselves without shame, and can live with themselves without conflict.

Much education and development has been supplied to modern leaders through the church, through the school, through the family, and through other segments of our society. Relatively few, however, have been trained to organize and codify these concepts into ethical guidelines for one's life— into philosophies.

It is the reaction of some that philosophies are more appropriately considered and discussed in academic and religious circles than in practical management. This hardly can be supported when it is realized that a philosophy is a basic attitude. It is a frame of mind. It is a guiding principle and should be a deep conviction. It is character!

Philosophies or basic attitudes are, therefore, what create the climate within which one's job is performed. They determine the nature of the action to be taken and how it is taken. They are the foundation of confidence in one's approach. They affect the people around us and have a great deal to do with their attitudes toward their own work and toward us.

Mediocrity vs. Excellence

Following the New York Yankee victory in the World Series of 1953, Red Smith, in his *New York Herald Tribune* column "Views of Sports," took exception to the rallying cry "Break Up the Yankees." It seems that the way most people approached the problem of enabling some other baseball club to win a pennant once in a while was to make the Yankees less powerful rather than to make the other teams better.

Red Smith said, " 'Break Up the Yankees' was a foolish slogan when it was coined and it set an unworthy goal. The aim should never be to destroy excellence, to bring the best down to the common level of mediocrity. Don't break up the Yankees, build up the others. Work harder, get better, and beat them."

This is a very sound philosophy and really is at the heart of professional management. When a company decries the excellence, power, and strength of a successful competitor and participates in all kinds of efforts to bring the competitor down to the complaining company's level, there is no contribution to progress in our economy. If, however, we set our sights toward becoming better than the competitor, we then have to plan exactly how we are going to do it and go about it in an orderly fashion.

The continuous and tiresome observation that the big company's experience and methods are not interesting or useful to the small company is defeating. The small company should make every effort to learn how the big company became what it is and what keeps it successful. There is nothing in the world that prohibits the small company from doing likewise.

The interesting and encouraging feature of our entire economy is that the successful organization seems perfectly willing to make its know-how available to others. The free exchange of experience among American businessmen is a source of amazement to the other countries of the world. When one studies the know-how of the successful organization, one will discover that success did not just happen—it was a result of good planning, good management, and big objectives.

Personal Philosophy

A personal philosophy should be thought out clearly and should consist of a firm foundation of convictions which guide our thought and activity. It becomes a summary of all the influences upon our lives from birth—our parents, homes, churches, educational institutions, employers, communities, governments, and friends.

The neurotics, the psychopathic cases, the frustrated, and the unstable are usually those who do not have a basic philosophy which stands up regardless of the successes or heartaches which life produces. A few years ago, AMA held a three-day seminar titled "Economic Education for Employees." The question arose as to what the average employee was seeking primarily. The conclusion seemed to be security.

The question then arose as to what constituted security. The consensus was that there is really no such thing as economic security. The only real security in the world is based upon two conditions: an individual can live with himself, and he possesses a skill which society needs and wants. This means that he is a stable, well-adjusted person; he knows what life is all about and what he wants to get out of it; and if he goes broke or loses his job tomorrow, he knows that his services will be demanded the next day.

Because personal philosophies vary with the convictions of the individual concerned, I am presenting here some of the questions that have to be answered in order to arrive at a philosophy. A philosophy has at least three parts. They deal with one's relationship with a supreme being, one's relationship with other individuals as individuals, and one's relationship with other individuals as members of a group. The first we call a *philosophy of life*. The second is called a *philosophy of work*. The third is called a *philosophy of society*.

Following are questions one has to answer to arrive at a philosophy of life: Do you believe there is a basic plan for civilization? Do you believe there is a supreme being, a divinity? Do you believe that the supreme being controls the plan of civilization? When you have answered these questions, you are well on the way toward determining your religion.

Following are questions one has to answer to arrive at a philosophy of work. Work is service to others. Whether one is digging a ditch, driving a truck, playing a piano in Carnegie Hall, or painting a masterpiece on canvas, he or she is working, doing something for someone else. Here are the questions: Do you believe that one who is mentally and physically able has an obligation to be of service to others? Do you believe that he who can work (be of service), but will not work, is entitled to receive any service from anybody else? In other words, do you believe such a person is entitled to any public assistance programs? Your answer to these questions will give you basis for much of your *political judgment*.

Here are questions to be answered about your philosophy of society: Do you believe an individual should surrender himself to the will of the group so the group may solve his problems for him? Do you believe that a group should benefit as each individual reaches his or her fullest potential? If you believe in the former, that is collectivism. If you believe in the latter, that is democracy. Now you have a basis for *social justice*.

In other words, if you are intellectually mature you have convictions that guide you in determining the difference between right and wrong. If you are emotionally stable, the difference between your convictions and your way of life is not very great. In order to determine what the difference is, you must organize your convictions into a philosophy by answering at least those questions just asked.

In Summary

It is imperative that today's leader, today's manager, should sit by the hour before an organization chart. On this chart should be the names of every member of his management, from himself to and including his first-line supervision. As he looks at each member of that team very intently, he should ask himself the following questions:

1. Is this person trained in the nature of management, the processes of management, and in what puts character into management?

2. Is this person knowledgeable about, trained and skilled in, the processes of management? Does he know what a manager does in order to act like a manager? Does he know how to determine what he wants people to do, what people he needs to do it, what physical resources he needs for these people, how well he wants the people to perform, how well they are performing, what can be done to get them to perform better, and what they should be paid if they do? Is he a master of the techniques and the tools that can be mastered only through specific training?

3. Is he showing, to any degree at all, those few basic characteristics that separate the men from the boys in management? What results is he attaining? Has he attained something significant? Does he have some kind of mission? Is it one that he and his followers respect? Does he practice consultative supervision? Is he intellectually mature and emotionally stable?

Until a chief executive has examined his entire management team in this way, and until he has provided the training, time, program, facilities, and money required to help his management people get this way, he is not fulfilling his responsibility. A leader's biggest job is to develop other leaders. The greatest test of leadership capability is the extent to which he can relax in the realization that his work is being done well by other people. This means that he is the leader of far more than he could personally handle and that he is insuring the growth and perpetuity of that mission to which he has been devoting his own life.

Chapter 9

THE SKILLS OF
MANAGEMENT IN
BROAD CATEGORIES

When we speak of management skills, the emphasis is on abilities rather than knowledge—abilities in managerial and administrative activities in contrast to those required in the technical, operating phases of a business. The skills of management are just as identifiable as those of any other profession, and they are peculiar to the management activity alone.

Maintaining the Economic Health of
an Organization

The ability to maintain the economic health of an organization is a skill of the greatest importance. In simple English, it means operating at a profit, with a surplus—staying in the black. There is a great deal of objection to and question about profits. There are those who maintain that profits in certain industries and companies are too large, but I have yet to find anyone who wants to work for an organization that does not make a profit. One can argue all he wishes as to whether a company is in business to make a profit, but he cannot argue at all with the fact that without profit, a company will not stay in business.

Something akin to righteous indignation rises within me when I hear it assumed that profit is undesirable, that the making of it is sinful, and that the fact that some individual can operate more profitably than another automatically establishes him as a crook. In the public mind, profit has tended to become a term of opprobrium, ranking high in the dictionary of epithets employed by the demagogue and the radical; a profitable corporation is considered by some to be an organization that follows undesirable practices.

The mere fact that Hitler used Wagnerian music to symbolize the "esthetic" side of his New Order is no reason why we should consign to the scrap heap some of the foremost works of musical literature. If a symbol has been abused, we must learn to look beyond it to the abuse itself.

So it is with profit. The freedom to make profit implies also the freedom to make it unfairly or to make it on products and services which, by many standards, are undesirable. This is inherent in the nature of freedom. With the freedom to do right, there must coexist the freedom to do wrong. Society, however, has a slow, certain way of dealing with those who are dishonest, ruthless, unfair, and who dispense what society considers harmful. While it must be recognized that profits have, at times, been made by exploitation and by anything but fair and acceptable management, the fact is that we are approaching the end of that era.

When a company receives more for the goods and services it produces and/or distributes than it has to disburse for the products and services it purchases, then that company is said to make a profit. If it continues to make such a profit over a long period of time, it may generally be inferred that society has placed the stamp of approval on the quality and methods of its products and services and, as a corollary, that the management of that company is sound and capable.

The overall profit made by a company is merely the sum total of the individual efforts of its many employees. The greater the number of individuals in the organization who produce more than they consume, the greater the profit of the company and of the individual employees themselves. Thus, the fundamental job of management is to increase the value of the contribution of each member of the organization—that is, to increase their productivity.

We have learned that productivity can be raised most effectively and most consistently when the methods used inspire the will and the desire to work and when the rewards are shared with all who contribute to the overall objective. In other words, the time has arrived or is very close at hand when the management which hopes to operate at a profit will do so only by employing those methods which inspire each and every worker to do his part. When the possibility of profit is eliminated or seriously curtailed, the desire for personal growth and for aiding the growth of others diminishes.

Government administration will always be more costly and less efficient than private management simply because there is no earned income in government and, therefore, no adequate opportunity for the public to express its judgment of the value of the services rendered. (A few government agencies do receive pay for services rendered, but they form an infinitesimal percentage of the overall government operation. There are those who will say that the ballot is an expression of the public's confidence in government administration, but no relationship exists between the general ballot box and the management of an individual government agency or bureau.) When the government's income does not offset what it pays for services rendered to it, it simply levies more taxes.

In brief, the income of government is not dependent upon the quality of its management.

Churches, hospitals, charitable and educational institutions, even though they are designated as nonprofit organizations, must operate with surpluses if they are to be successful. They win financial support by the kind of service they render—the better the service, the greater the support. If more of them functioned on that concept, they could boast far better administration. Too many such institutions are under the misconception that the public is obligated to maintain them, regardless of how poorly operated they are.

Profit, savings surplus—they are all one and the same—are still measures of management. When they are interpreted as an indication of services rendered to society which are greater than those received from society, then they remain a noble and basic objective of management. They mean that the management involved is successful in helping the members of the organization provide more for others than they demand from others.

Maintaining the economic health of an organization is a management skill, and that manager who does not have it need not be deeply concerned about the possession of the other skills listed below. He will not be around very long.

Integrating the Viewpoints of People and Functions

When we recall the differences in the backgrounds of people which result in no two individuals being alike, and when we think of all of the departmental activities as well as geographical divisions and subdivisions of an organization to which the experience and loyalties of company people are often restricted, we begin to see what a job it is to integrate all these viewpoints, ideas, and allegiances. It takes great skill to do this without curbing individual initiative or undermining important loyalties to particular segments of an organization. At the same time, we want full participation in the betterment of the business for the good of all.

This is the skill which enables a manager to make a team out of a group. This is the ability which reduces strife between line and staff positions and causes both to understand that they have equally important parts to play—even though the parts are completely different. This is where coordination and integration become the major considerations. The marketer has to understand the problems of the manufacturer and give him adequate information and notice of change in demand. The manufacturer has to comprehend the quality, quantity, and delivery needs of the marketer. The financial executive has to appreciate that a business is not a banking institution and that money has to be put to work and kept at work, while at the same time there must be adequate cash to do business. The accountant has to appreciate that the business is not functioning in order to maintain accounting records, but that accounting records are for the purpose of helping the business progress toward the attainment of its objectives.

It is the increasing problem of integrating viewpoints and functions that is causing the great current interest in better methods of communication. How can we comprehend what the other fellow is trying to say and what his interests are? How can we get him to comprehend our problems and hopes? How can we combine the two in the best interests of the company, where individual interests and desires have to take second place?

We have heard a lot over the years about two-way communication—both up and down. We are now beginning to hear about three-way communication—the third way being horizontal. Departments and divisions of an organization become too segregated and isolated. The lawyer has something to contribute to the rest of the business other than just legal opinions. The engineer is an intelligent, educated, and experienced man and has some judgment on matters other than those requiring engineering know-how. The personnel administrator ought to be deeply interested in problems of the business other than human problems and should be deeply concerned about them. The sales manager frequently has very helpful suggestions in relation to manufacturing, and vice versa.

There are many basic fundamental patterns to the organization structure of the General Electric Company, which was instituted by Ralph Cordiner a few years after he became president. One of these fundamentals was his description of the basic responsibilities of his chief executives. Each of them had two major jobs: to run the particular department or operating functions for which he was specifically held responsible; and to serve as a member of a group which, with the president, was responsible for the entire General Electric Company. That means that each executive must operate his own particular responsibility in terms of what is good for the company as a whole. He is jointly responsible with the president for the success of the entire business, as well as for his own particular segment of it.

Unfortunately, there is a great deal of argument and misunderstanding about the use of committees. There are extreme viewpoints—all the way from the chief executive who will have no committees of any kind in his organization to another executive who runs his entire business through the committee form of organization. This is largely due to the fact that the functions of committees are not clearly understood and they are frequently misused.

Committees never were intended to be decision-making or operating bodies—as far as business and industrial organization is concerned. Someone once observed that Lindbergh never could have flown the Atlantic by committee. The main purpose of a committee is to integrate the viewpoints of people and functions. It is an excellent educational, informational, and advisory device. It is a medium by which an executive can secure the suggestions and opinions of all people involved before he arrives at a particular course of action.

This is a distinct skill and it is peculiar to the leadership function. It deserves conscious attention on the part of every manager, and he should be a student of every device and tool available to him which will enable him to make a team of a group of individual stars.

Instilling the Service Motive

This involves the skill to put that extra fire into an organization—that plus which enables it to win when the chips are down, which causes it to get through a crisis, which enables it to do more than anyone anticipated it could do. It is what Casey Stengel, former manager of the New York Yankees, was referring to when he said, "Something happens to a ball player when you put a Yankee uniform on him." It is filling the hearts, minds, and souls of the individuals in an organization with the belief that what they are doing is important enough to do well, and that there is every reason in the world to believe that they can do it better than anybody else can.

Some of the most fascinating and constructive discussions that a group of executives can have within a business are those which are directed toward clarification and definition of why the company is in business. Invariably, the first conclusion is "to make a profit." Complete and adequate discussion, however, frequently leads to another conclusion.

A business usually starts with an idea. The idea normally is a product or a service. Sufficient capital to start and finance the business in its early days is made available in accordance with the strength and value of the idea. The business grows and progresses in accordance with consumer and investor acceptance. This means that an organization primarily makes a product or line of products which society needs and wants. In order to do this and do it successfully, the organization has to make a profit. Profit thereby becomes a means to an end and not an end in itself.

It is quite difficult to inspire an organization with the narrow objective of making a profit so that investors of money, time, and effort may themselves have more money. Money is a practical incentive but it has seldom proved adequate to fire men's souls.

Those who create a serious issue over whether a company is in business to make a profit or render a service usually have not taken the time to think the matter through adequately. Experience over the years has proved that when they do give it some thought, they get profit in its proper perspective and, as a result, make more of it.

If an organization is dedicated to the rendering of a significant service to the consumer, every job in the organization should make a contribution toward that end. Every person in every job should be made to realize the importance of the contribution of his job. If the janitor, the elevator operator, the porter, or the clerk in the shipping room is not performing a job which ultimately contributes to the quality of the service rendered by the organization, then the job should not exist. There are managers who can make every person on the team feel he is performing the most important contribution to the ultimate goals attained by the team, and that is a skill.

The president's chauffeur is frequently the proudest and "most important" man in the organization so far as he is concerned. He is looking out for every convenience and comfort of the president, trying to save him time, and trying to keep him in a good frame of mind. That is important to the welfare of the entire organization.

During World War II, one of the great cities of this nation had to be classified by the War Manpower Commission as a No. 1 critical area. That meant that that city was unable to meet its war production schedules and, therefore, no more contracts could be placed there until the city could get out the production for which it was obligated. In this particular case, the major cause of the situation was a shortage of manpower.

A citizen's committee of management, government, and labor was organized in order to move people voluntarily from nonessential to essential work and to get people to work full-time or part-time who were not working at all. Every known device was used—newspapers, radio, sound trucks, rallies, station wagons going from door to door, and so forth.

In the course of this great campaign, twenty-four girls walked into the U.S. Employment Service office in a group. They asked for war jobs. The clerk soon discovered that they were all working in the same place and asked them where it was. In response, they named the radar plant which was No. 1 on the priority list into which the city was trying to get workers!

Your first reaction could reasonably be that this is impossible. Consider if you will, however, the backgrounds of these girls. They probably lived alone or with a roommate. They went from their rooms to work on the same bus every day. Probably, all they read was comic strips and all they listened to on the radio was soap operas, and probably ever since they had worked in the plant they had been checked in at the gate, had badges hung on them, and had no reason to know that that was just a war measure and not something that had been going on for fifty years.

The experience of these girls and the world in which they lived were very restricted. They had no way of knowing they were working on radar equipment. There are those who said you could not tell them for security reasons. For my money, that is a lot of eyewash. Anybody who wanted to know, knew that radar was made in that plant. There was no reason why those girls could not have been told that the little spools they were winding thread on all day long went into radar sets for which fully equipped and manned warships were standing in New York and San Francisco harbors waiting in order to get into action. It would not have changed the

115

course of the war one iota for these girls to know it, and it certainly would have instilled in them an important service motive.

Firing up an organization to a fighting pitch is more than group stimulation. It rests upon the skill to make every individual member of the group appreciate that what he or she is doing is extremely valuable to the rendering of an important service.

Making an Organization Dynamic and Adaptable

The skill to make an organization dynamic and adaptable may seem, on the face of it, to be closely related to instilling the service motive. It is not, however, *exactly* the same. While a dynamic organization must have the service motive, that, in itself, will not make it dynamic. What we are talking about here is the skill to put together a team which is carefully selected—one in which each person is well qualified, sharply trained, clearly assigned, and competently led. It can be described as a tight, taut, hard-hitting organization which possesses a high degree of morale.

Adaptability means that the organization is able to adjust itself quickly to changing conditions; it is flexible. This means that the team is trained in the T formation and the single- and double-wing formations, as well as in the L formation. It means that it can play a five-, seven-, or nine-man defense, according to what the competition's offense is. It means that it can quickly sense what is needed and shift its defense or its attack without disintegration, panic, or confusion.

There are many arguments in favor of stability and comfort. There is much opposition to change. As a result, organizations that are progressive leaders at one time can find themselves, a few years later, dropping lower in competitive position and dying of obsolescence and complacency. Human beings are not static but are ever changing; everything around us reflects that. Nothing is static. The status quo is an unattainable position. The proud driver of the newest and latest model automobile today is envious of his neighbor's car two years from today. His car that was so beautiful is now out of style.

Keeping an organization flexible, adaptable, and dynamic is a skill requiring conscious attention, and the results cannot be left to chance. The public does not continue to support an organization that no longer meets its needs and standards even though at one time they may have cheered it as the champion.

Providing Human Satisfactions from Work Output and Relations

There is every indication that when Thomas Jefferson wrote the Declaration of Independence, he had been reading the works of John Locke, the British economist and philosopher. Locke wrote an essay on the purpose of the state in which he listed as one of the purposes the protection of life, liberty, and property. There is evidence that the first copy of the Declaration of Independence which Thomas Jefferson wrote had in it "the inalienable right to life, liberty, and property." Jefferson must have reconsidered. He must have recalled why people came to this land of ours, and arrived at the conclusion that property is a means to an end rather than an end in itself. He therefore used the phrase "the inalienable right to life, liberty, and the pursuit of happiness." Happiness, therefore, becomes the objective.

Everyone has his own opinion as to what is the greatest source of happiness. I happen to believe that it is satisfaction of the basic desire to create something. Human beings fundamentally want their lives to be of value and they want to create something that makes that so. That, I believe, is the fundamental reason why a man wants a home. It is not just to have a roof over his head and a place to eat and sleep, but it is to have an institution which exerts an influence upon the lives of others. The community should be better because of his home; the people who are in it should be better because of the atmosphere that has been created. He is the head of the home; it is his; it is a great source of pride and satisfaction.

Unfortunately, many people work simply in order to earn the means by which they can attain certain satisfactions out of living. It is by far a healthier situation if an individual can obtain a certain amount of satisfaction out of work itself and the work environment.

This skill of providing certain human satisfactions in work output and relations is closely related to that of instilling the service motive. The service motive certainly helps to provide satisfactions out of the type of work produced, but it does not completely provide what is essential in work relations. The kind of physical environment in which a person works, the kind of people with whom he works, the type of leadership which he enjoys, the benefits which he receives, are all ingredients of work relations.

Where the management is deeply concerned about and interested in each individual in the organization, where the workers are congenial, interested in, and loyal to each other, and where all of this takes place in a climate of mutual confidence and respect, then a lot of human satisfaction can be obtained from our workday.

This is one of the major reasons being given by companies who are currently moving out of the cities with their plants and offices. Recently, I was in a city in the South and was driven around within a fifty-mile area of that city. I was amazed at the beautiful new plants, thirty-five of which had been constructed within the last five years. As I drive about the environs of New York City, I see a very active move to locate businesses physically in more pleasant working and living conditions.

When one talks with the executives who are responsible

for these shifts from city to country, invariably the first answer you get is that they wanted to find a decent place to live, work, and bring up their children. There is plenty of room for varied opinions as to what kinds of locations meet these conditions, and that is good. What is important, however, is that working conditions are becoming a matter of major concern. This indicates an active attempt to increase the human satisfactions derived from work situations.

This skill, like many others, involves a basic attitude as well as an ability. I understand from my Quaker friends that they have a rather common expression or question which they ask each other: "Has thee a concern?" That is a pretty good attitude to have as a foundation for this whole problem—are you concerned about it?

Relating the Company's Affairs to the Community

There are in my possession at the moment two statements of company policies on the same subject. One says: "Any employee of this company who participates in any organized activity outside of the company without specific permission from the president is subject to immediate dismissal." The other policy states: "The Board of Directors of this company sees no good reason why its employees should not participate in the recognized and accepted activities of the community in which we exist and upon whose strength we depend for our continued existence." One cannot read these two diametrically opposed viewpoints without realizing that there must be a noticeable difference in the character of the two institutions.

The skill of relating the activities of a company to those of a community starts with the declaration of the company's basic attitude. The people of an organization must know whether their management encourages, condones, or prohibits their participation in community affairs. Still further skill is required to control such activities without discouraging them. Obviously, employees could and do become so active in community affairs that it materially affects their performance on the job. Some are just plain joiners. It takes skill to control this wisely and still fulfill community responsibilities.

Any management which believes that it can operate a business independently of the community in which it exists is living with its head in the sand. Any business operating within the limits of a particular locality is dependent upon that locality for good schools, churches, hospitals, and other service institutions of this kind. They determine the character of the community and the people who live in it—who, in turn, work for the company involved. An executive must appreciate this and be able to get it in proper perspective.

The Henry Lawrence Gantt Medal, awarded annually by the American Society of Mechanical Engineers and the American Management Associations, is presented to an executive who is recognized for "distinguished achievement in industrial management as a service to the community." The recipients of this medal over the last thirty-five years include such personalities as Henry S. Dennison, Arthur H. Young, William L. Batt, Lillian and Frank Gilbreth, John M. Hancock, Paul G. Hoffman, Alvin E. Dodd, Charles R. Hook, Clarence Francis, Ralph J. Cordiner, Frederick R. Kappel, and Robert E. Brooker. These are individuals who have been publicly recognized as possessing the skill to relate their activities to those of the community. For further elaboration as to what this means, just read the life stories of these people.

"Community" is used here in its broadest sense. It starts, of course, at the local level and then expands to the county, state, federal, and international communities. There is no businessman in America today unaffected by international affairs. Even though there may be some who are isolationist in belief they cannot avoid the impact of what is going on throughout the entire world.

Chapter 10

A PLAN OF MANAGEMENT

A program is a "plan for future action." A plan of management is that which managers follow in directing the activities for which they are held responsible. Such a plan does not specify *what* is to be managed, but rather *how* any operation may be managed.

If supervisors and executives have a definite program or method of management which they follow, they have planned their attack upon the activities and problems of the future, regardless of what these may be. They are conscious that the events of the future can, to some extent, be influenced, controlled, and even created. A large part of their success depends upon the degree to which they plan the direction of the forces which influence, control, and create future events.

A plan of management would not appeal to or be of interest to those individuals who are inclined to let things work rather than make them work—individuals who are inclined to let things come as they may, rather than to influence how or when they come, or prevent their arrival.

Many are inclined to *let* organizations work rather than to *make* them work. Due to the inherent ability of human beings, such leadership often gets by. Those organizations live, however, in spite of their leadership, not because of it. Many of us are inclined to let democracy work rather than to make it work. If those who are a part of democracy would put one-half the effort into making it work that those who are promoting various "isms" put into *their* plans, there is not a single form of government that could challenge democracy.

In other words, a definite program or plan of management is a challenge to dynamic leadership—to men and women who wish to exert an influence upon the future of their organizations. It evokes the best in any person in an executive or supervisory capacity. It is a relatively simple matter to find people who can sit on a job, handle events as they come, meet emergencies, and get by. It is difficult to find individuals who can plan, who can make events happen as they want them to happen, who, through such planning, can reduce emergencies, and who can keep their organizations in positions of leadership.

The real power of management is its capacity to make things happen that otherwise would not happen. It is management that forecasts, sets the plans, mobilizes and directs the organization toward the attainment of those plans. If management makes up its mind to do something and then approaches it in a planned and rational way, there is no limit to the future of our economy. Any plan of management is better than no plan at all.

Efficiency and Morale

The entire management activity of planning should be directed toward the development of conditions that create good morale, both individual and group. They happen to be much the same conditions that create greater efficiency. *Efficiency as an objective is an evil, but as a byproduct of good morale, it is a just reward.*

Since all organizations are made up of human beings, and since all human beings have weaknesses, organizations will always reflect the shortcomings of the people who make them up. Any individual with an average education and a fair amount of common sense can study an organization and fill a voluminous report with descriptions of conditions that are not what they ought to be. The individual does not live, however, who can study an organization and, in six months or a year, tell you all the things that are wrong with it *and* the proper methods by which all of these wrongs may be righted.

There are within any organization the intelligence, the experience, and the ability to discover what is wrong with operations and also to discover ways and means by which those conditions can be corrected, provided the management will give the members of the organization the time and the means to express themselves along these lines. A planned management approach simply shows the way by which this can be done. It does not supply the answers; it shows how those answers may be obtained. It does not specifically endorse any particular type of organization or technical method of doing a job; it simply indicates to the people concerned how they may discover the best kind of organization and the best possible methods for their particular situation.

Planning vs. Approval

Many executives complain that they are too busy to plan. A question just as old as "Which came first, the hen or the egg?" is: "How busy should an executive be?" There are those who believe that the proper executive atmosphere is that of long hours, missed lunches, batteries of telephones, last-minute travel reservations, dictating machines by the bedside, and the like. There are others who say that the best executive is the one who never appears to be rushed or busy; who can do his work within the limits of office hours; who has the time to discuss anything with anybody; who delegates all responsibility, and can occasionally play golf without fear of the business falling apart in his absence. Agreement on the answer to that question probably will never be reached because management is largely a matter of personalities and not systems. There probably is a medium ground between the two viewpoints that comes more nearly to being correct than either of the extremes presented.

There are, however, some features of executive practice which seem to meet general approval. One is that the number of items or activities that a manager has to sign or approve can be greatly overdone. There are men who believe that a real executive job is stting at a desk signing and approving. The number of times a man has to sign his name does not indicate the extent of his importance.

A principle which is fairly well accepted is that *authority should be delegated within definitely defined limits.* Some people do not delegate authority because they have not established limits for the control of authority and each individual case has to be considered on its own merits. There are some managers, for example, who maintain that authority for salary changes cannot be delegated. Their feeling is that all salary changes should be approved by a salary committee or some executive of high standing. Such managers usually do not have any established salary-group limits within which changes are made. If time is taken to establish income limits for each job—maximums and minimums—then it is a simple matter to delegate authority to any executive or to any supervisor to administer salary changes within those established limits.

These limits, within which authority can be granted, should be written into policy. The development of policy on a sound basis would build the road upon which we are to travel, and we would have the privilege of traveling on that road in any kind of vehicle and at any speed we wish to, just so long as we stay on the road and reach our destination at the established time.

In other words, the better the administrative planning, the better the policies and the fewer executive approvals required. When management properly establishes objectives, procedures, and responsibilities in connection with the major activities of the operation, more time is available for further planning and greater perfection in present planning.

The complaint continues from many sources that executives and supervisors do not have time to do long-range planning because each day brings more than enough duties to fill the day. Somehow, sometime, we must neglect a day's duties, or get somebody else to do them, so as to have time to establish the course for tomorrow before the ship strikes a shoal.

The Executive Function

All of this presentation can be summed up in this way. An executive, or manager, whichever you wish to call him, is supposed to:

1. Determine what he wants people to do.
2. Select and train the most qualified people he can to do it.
3. Check periodically to see how well they are doing it.
4. See that methods are found by which they can do better.
5. Discipline them. (Discipline has two aspects to it: reward for work well done, and appropriate treatment for failure.)

Anything else that a manager is doing is not management.

Chapter 11

MANAGEMENT THE
SIMPLE WAY

Once I wrote a book that followed all the rules: It had an impressive, all-inclusive title; it had a preface, an introduction, an index; it contained research references, appendix, and bibliography; and between its covers were the findings of some fifteen years' experience with staff and line executives, top and middle management, supervisors, foremen, and lead men.

The book suffered, however, from at least one common weakness—it made a simple, natural process appear complicated and difficult. The result was that many of those who might have profited by it did not finish it, while those who did finish it were too confounded by the apparent complexity of the subject to act on many of the recommendations.

Is it not odd how men and women like to complicate and distort simple, natural activities? Why do we fight the

EDITORIAL NOTE: This chapter first appeared as an article in *Personnel* magazine in January 1943. Since it is the author's first—and perhaps still his most cogent—statement of the basic management ideas contained in this book, it is reprinted here with only slight changes.

obvious? Why do we insist upon flying in the face of facts and principles which have been tested and proved over the years? Why do we continue to insist that we are different, that the people with whom we deal are different, that the activities in which we are engaged and the problems with which we are faced are different? Why do we continue to demand special consideration and tailor-made treatment? All we accomplish is to make things difficult for ourselves and unpleasant for those around us.

No automobile is exactly the same as another. Most automobiles look different; they have varied origins; they operate in multiple environments, perform numerous functions, and are used in many geographic areas and under normal and extreme climatic conditions. But they all work on the same principles: Their engines will stop without fuel; their parts will break down without proper care; their tires will go flat if punctured. No one of them will perform in the same way for different drivers, and no two of them respond alike for the same driver. Sailboats are like that too. So are people. They all operate according to the same basic principles, and all have individual personalities.

The Simplest Way of All

We think of the Gettysburg Address as a masterpiece of simplicity, but there is a much older pronouncement which by comparison makes the Gettysburg Address look like a Federal income tax statement. The modernized version is, "Do unto others as you would have them do unto you."

There, in one sentence, is the greatest book ever written, on the greatest subject there is, by the greatest author that ever lived. There is the main principle of good management in its simplest form. Why do we need more? Why do we require tons of books to explain something so simple?

It can only be because of our stubborn human desire

to write the rules our own way. "Do unto others what we think ought to be done." That version of the rule opens the door to all our selfish motives. It warps our judgments, creates economic depressions, gives rise to pressure groups, loses wars. It causes us to hold tenaciously to pet prejudices, outworn traditions, antiquated practices, and valueless, time-consuming procedures. It creates duplication of effort, induces neglect of responsibilities, fosters misunderstandings and jealousies, and makes for friction and lost time. In other words, it makes a simple job difficult. *When prejudice and selfishness enter, reason, justice, and simplicity exit.*

Leadership—A Natural Process

There has been so much written about "executive abilities," "administrative talents," and "managerial qualifications," and there have been so many arguments about whether leaders are born or made, that the whole field of leadership has been engulfed in mysticism. As a result, many actual and potential managers develop fear complexes and imagine complicated situations where none exist.

The truth of the matter is that leadership is a perfectly natural status in life. The world divides itself casually into leaders and followers. In any situation, such a division takes place, and no one can stop it. Civilization is bound to progress (assuming you have any faith in a supreme plan for the universe), and progress depends upon leadership.

The situation is complicated somewhat, however, because some of us feel that the whole future of the world depends upon us—that if we do not bring about perfection during our regimes the world is doomed. If we would only stop to realize that competent people contributed to world progress long before our time and that there are capable people still to be born, we would be more sympathetic toward the idea of leaving something for posterity to do.

Let us each make his own contribution with as little fuss and feathers as possible and in a simple and natural way. This does not mean we should work any less hard, but it does mean that there is little merit in being busy just for the sake of being busy. *Activity is of value only in terms of attainment.*

Management and Human Development

It would seem that we should be convinced by now that the success of any organization depends on having an adequate number of human beings in the right jobs at the right time, all producing at their highest capacity—outstanding people have told us so often enough. Then why do many of us expect intelligent human relations to develop spontaneously, while most of our time and effort is devoted to consideration of production schedules, transportation facilities, availability of raw materials, prices, and markets?

It complicates management activity to a great degree when a struggle is necessary to place personnel activities on the same level of importance in the minds of operating officials as material items. Whenever consideration of the human element has a place other than of primary importance in management circles, ultimate success of the organization is made more difficult.

Management has been defined in very simple terms as "getting things done through the efforts of other people," and that function breaks down into at least two major responsibilities, one of which is planning, the other control.

Planning encompasses the whole field of deciding what you want human beings to accomplish. This involves the careful determination of needs, the establishment of objectives, the outlining of procedures that will attain those objectives, and the proper assignment of responsibility to individuals or groups of individuals.

If it is impossible to build a house without a blueprint, without some indication of what the carpenters, electricians, masons, plumbers, and painters are to do, how can we expect to manufacture a product or render a service without the same careful planning?

Control requires the use of various media which will impel the people in the organization to work in accordance with the plan. There are at least two control factors that require careful attention: One is organization structure, and the other is supervision.

Unless the *organization structure* is simple and unless all who are part of it understand it, it will defeat its own purpose, which is to enable people to work together in groups as effectively as they would work alone. If there is misunderstanding about individual and/or departmental authority and responsibility, or about interrelationships between individuals and organization units, people cannot work effectively.

The function of *supervision* is to close the gaps between desired performance and actual human performance. If the mere issuance of policies and instructions would induce people to do what they are supposed to do, supervision would not be necessary.

Having divided the activity of management into the two basic elements of planning and control, it is simple to arrive at a statement of the primary executive function—*to determine what you want people to accomplish, to check periodically on how well they are accomplishing it, to find and train people competent for such accomplishment, to see that methods are developed by which they will perform more effectively, and to discipline them.*

This all leads us to a rather simple truth: *Management is the development of people and not the direction of things.* If this fact were more generally accepted, many management difficulties would disappear. The executive or supervisor who says that he would rather exhaust himself doing things correctly than expend the time and patience necessary to get other people to do them correctly is admitting that he cannot manage.

From these deductions it is not difficult to comprehend the fact that management and personnel administration are one and the same. They should never be separated. Management is personnel administration.

Since management requires staff and line activities, it is natural to divided personnel functions between staff and line executives, providing one appreciates the significance of each. Line executives have complete and final responsibility for personnel matters and final authority for them. Staff personnel executives are expected to advise, help, and be of service to the line in the fulfillment of these responsibilities. There is an important place for both in any administrative setup.

What complicates an otherwise simple matter is the desire on the part of some operating executives to delegate all personnel responsibility to a staff personnel executive and/or department as well as the desire on the part of some personnel executives to seize such responsibility. If this is permitted, the human element cannot receive proper consideration.

Simple Human Desires and Motives

Consumer acceptance of products or services is dependent upon public good will—that is a well-accepted truism. It is also axiomatic that public good will is influenced the most by the employees of the organization—those who are selling the products or rendering the services. *Good employee relations within an organization are, therefore, the most important contributing factor to a sound and successful business.*

If you are to build sound employee relations, your dealings with the human beings in your organization must take into account the perfectly natural, simple motives and desires of those human beings. To clarify that point, let us consider a few of these natural interests. As they are presented, think of yourself as the employee. If you agree that they apply to you personally, you can rest assured that they apply to every worker under your direction.

1. *When an individual is seeking a new connection, he likes to be treated courteously and made to feel at home and at ease.* Under such conditions, he can be natural and show himself to the best advantage. That means that the individual seeking a job does not like to be herded down some back alley into a drab cell of an employment office. And when he arrives there, he does not like to be treated like a criminal in the line-up at police headquarters. The prospective employee's contact with the employment office is his first impression of the organization for which he may be working in a few days. In the atmosphere of an employment office, you sow the first seeds of morale.

2. *The average individual likes to be welcomed to a job rather than thrown into it.* Without much effort, simple induction procedures and orientation training can be provided. Such a program makes the new employee feel that he is considered an entity of some value, not a nonproductive nuisance. The average person does not like to be shoved at an unsympathetic foreman, who in turn hands him over to some skilled mechanic to whom a greenhorn is a pest. Yet new workers are receiving such treatment every day.

3. *The ordinary human being would like to receive simple and intelligent instruction in what he is expected to do, how it can be done, and what constitutes a job well done.* A simple program of job instruction which will enable the new employee to master his own job and prepare himself for a better one is not hard to devise. Agreement on what constitutes a job well done can be brought about by the establishment of simple standards of performance, in terms of quantity, quality, time, cost, and tests to be met. Working without standards is like participating in an athletic contest without any system of scoring.

4. *Any human being likes to work under someone whom he can respect and in whom he can have confidence.* The greatest single morale-builder is the feeling of the part of a worker, "I like to work for that man." To foster that feeling, capable supervision is necessary. But intelligent, capable supervision can be developed only through a management-planned and -administered program of continuous supervisory training. This also is a simple practice which pays big dividends.

5. *Every individual likes someone to recognize his or her importance.* One of the simple driving motives in human nature is the desire to have a place in the sun. A management which recognizes that each individual on the payroll has some intelligence, some ability, and something to contribute to the company's policies and operations—no matter how small the contribution may be—has satisfied a basic desire. Human beings like to be heard, and they like to have their opinions and suggestions considered and respected. Channels of communication between top management and employees will, if established and kept open, contribute toward this end. Conferences, personal contacts between supervisors and employees, suggestion systems, house organs, and the like are all simple methods of establishing such channels. An intelligent grievance procedure, which gives any employee the right to reach top management, is essential.

6. *Many human beings like to feel their daily work is of service to others.* In fact, the greater the opportunity for service, and the more the employee realizes it, the less the demand for material recognition. Knowledge of the organization involved—its objectives, policies, accomplishments, management philosophy, and the part each worker plays in them—all help to satisfy this natural human desire.

7. *There are few human beings who do not desire realistic recognition of a job well done.* We all like to be paid what the work we do is worth, and in accordance with employer capacity to pay. We all like to receive promotions

when our abilities and merits justify them. Simple systems of job evaluation, salary and wage administration, merit rating, and job progression would satisfy this desire. Why are they not in greater use?

8. *There are few human beings who will not work hard and long for incentive.* Special recognition always inspires greater effort. A pat on the back has its merits, but a medal on the uniform is tangible evidence of management appreciation. Special awards, bonuses, prizes, etc., fairly administered, increase the desire to produce. Why do we try to complicate such simple things as incentives? Why do we try to level off rewards, to treat everyone alike, regardless of attainment? Why do we do so when we know that a simple human impulse is to produce more when more recognition is possible?

9. *Every human being likes to work in an organization in which there is universal confidence in the ability and fairness of top management.* Most people who are worth their salt will go through hell for a leader in whom they believe. They will put up with anything because of their confidence in him. A management which is frank and above-board, which has in it no vestige of paternalism, which is fair and open in its business and labor negotiations, will satisfy this inherent desire. Management reports to employees, personal contacts during which management and employees come to know each other as personalities, are simple means to this end.

10. *All of us want to be sound of mind and body.* Consequently it helps when others take an interest in our health, and particularly when our managers do—we cannot work well when mentally or physically ill. Vacations with pay, medical examinations and services, hospitalization plans, safety programs, credit unions, employee counseling, all help the employee to keep well. Incidentally, they will pay dividends in increased production and improved morale.

11. *A basic instinct in all of us is the desire for security.* When a human being is worried about his job or about the welfare of those dependent on him, he cannot produce effec-

tively. We all know that our earning capacity is certain to diminish eventually, and the fear of want in old age is constantly before us. Annuity plans, insurance programs, opportunities for savings, job stability, all help to counteract this fear. And they are all possible if we but have the will to create them.

12. *When it is necessary for an employee to terminate relations with an employer, he likes to do so with his head in the air and with a full understanding of the reasons for termination.* He does not like to be notified of his termination by a pink slip attached to his time card. If termination is for cause, he does not like some mushy-mouthed, smooth-acting diplomat to lie to him. A properly conducted and timed exit interview would, in most cases, satisfy his normal wish to know the facts.

These, then, are some simple truths about human beings. Added up, they make plain, everyday horse sense. So why do we tend to make them needlessly complicated?

Seven Simple Steps to Good Management

If one were to summarize all the different ways of insuring good management that have been suggested over the years, the list would run into the hundreds. But it would be of little value because the average operating executive or supervisor would probably take one look at it and decide that the whole matter was too complicated to act upon in one short lifetime.

In the interest of simplicity, a few steps are outlined at this point. If followed carefully and with reasonable attention to sequence, they will insure adequate management attention to the way in which operations are conducted. With both old and new employees and in both old and new situations, application of these recommendations will bring about improvement in human performance.

1. (With the person involved) *Develop a simple outline of the functions and operations to be performed.* This can apply to an individual job or to any complete unit of an organization. It should include an understandable statement of what people are to do, what authority they have in doing it, and what their relationships with other people are.

2. (With the person involved) *Develop a simple statement of results which will be considered satisfactory.* There are many activities for which, at first, it seems impossible to develop standards of performance. However, discussion of them in a sincere attempt to develop standards will often produce very definite and acceptable objectives.

3. (With the person involved) *At regular intervals, check actual performance against the standards that have been set.* If management is to plan its activities, it must know how big a gap there is between what is being done and what should be done. This should be checked in terms of individual and group attainment.

4. (With the person involved) *Make a list of corrective actions necessary to improve performance where such improvement is needed.* An individual cannot develop into a better worker and a better citizen unless he is continuously increasing his skill, gaining knowledge, changing his habits, and assuming constructive attitudes. A manager should know where improvement is needed.

5. (With the person involved) *Select the best sources from which he can obtain help and information.* Sources can be divided into four categories: the immediate supervisor, other individuals in the organization, people outside the organization who could be brought in, and outside sources of help to which the individuals concerned could be referred. These sources should be considered in that order, and the one which is the most advantageous selected.

6. (With the person involved) *A time should be set aside in advance for supplying the help and information that is needed.* If we do not plan in advance, the time can be made

available only through disrupting the functioning of the organization. It is of little use to go to all the trouble of deciding what should be done, analyzing what has been done, and determining what action is needed, if no action is taken.

7. (With the person involved) *Arrive at mutual agreement as to what constitutes a fair day's pay for a fair day's work, as well as what nonfinancial incentives are worth working for.* On a firm base of fairly administered financial rewards, a climate can be developed that will cause people to stay with you rather than go elsewhere for more money.

No specific system of carrying out these recommendations is needed. *Method* is relatively unimportant if a continuous attempt is made by intelligent people to do what is suggested.

It seems a simple and natural conclusion that the people in the organization should receive as much attention as material items. If this were done in a conscious, orderly way rather than in haphazard and spasmodic bursts of enthusiasm, the results would be astounding.

Improvement—Not Perfection

It is an interesting commentary on human nature that many of us must see a new project spelled out in detail before we attempt it. We then argue about the details and sometimes refuse to take action because we cannot see how to cross every bridge in advance. If those in positions of responsibility would determine the fundamental "rightness" of a proposition and then with unshakable faith in that judgment move on to find the way, human progress would be more rapid than it is now. There is so much argument about methods and techniques that the question of basic "rightness" or "wrongness" is sometimes overlooked.

Perfection in any activity can be attained only through practice. If no one had been willing to fly the original airplane because it was not a perfect mechanism, where would air transportation be today? What we are flying today is probably not nearly as good as the planes ten years from now will be. The same is true of management methods of dealing with the human element.

It is said of General Pershing that during World War I when one of the members of his staff complained that a certain officer at the front was making many mistakes, his reaction was, "That's right, but he's making them fast." He who makes no mistakes makes no progress. He who makes progress without mistakes is not human.

If what is outlined here seems reasonable and sound and if we have faith enough in it to make a start on some of those things from which we have shied away, we are in for some pleasant management experiences. A human being reacts quickly and favorably to understanding, fairness, and consideration. If we approach our management activities with the idea of doing things in the simple, natural way, much of the confusion and frustration which we now experience will disappear.

The greatest single reward which any manager, supervisor, foreman, or lead man can receive is to have those who have been under his direction say that they are better workers, better citizens, and better producers because of his leadership. Such an attitude builds morale and loyalty, and these will accomplish the impossible.